MW01285251

"FINDING FAITH"

(Part II "The Faith" Series)

THE FAITH SERIES

SERIES #1

SERIES #2

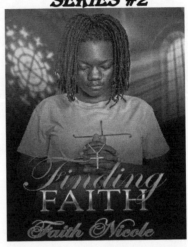

SERIES #3

SERIES #4

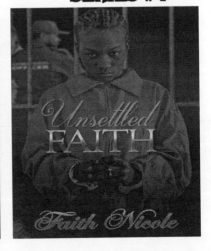

Finding Faith
~Written BY~
Faith Nicole

Copyright © 2019 by Faith Nicole
Facebook: *Faith Nicole*
FB Group: *Purple Diamonds Inc*
Instagram: *Purple Diamonds Inc*
Email: *refusetolosefaith@gmail.com*
Website: *purplediamondsinc.com*
YouTube: *Purple Diamonds Inc*

All rights reserved by the author Faith Nicole. No part of this book may be reproduced, copied, stored, or transmitted in any form or by any means,---graphic, electronic, or mechanical, including photocopying, recording, or information storage and retrieval systems---without the prior written permission of Faith Nicole Publications, LLC.

Cover Design: Tina Louise

This novel is inspired by actual events. However, names, characters, and incidents has been changed to protect all parties involved.

ACKNOWLEDGEMENTS

Thank You Heavenly Father for blessing me with the ability to transition my thoughts & feelings into words. Thank You for Your Love, Grace, Mercy, & Divine Connections. & thank You for loving me enough to see the good in me, even when I could not see it in myself.

Thank you Kim for being the listening ear & brutal truth I needed. & for always keeping me encouraged & uplifted.

Thank you Author Willie Mack for taking me under your wing & educating me. Because of you, my publishing process was easier than I expected.

Thank you Author Chatrivia Unique for showing me that it's okay to live your truth. You are a great inspiration, & the laughs, well they were just bonuses.

Thank you Temper Tantrum Tina for professionally photographing & designing my book covers. You gave me exactly what I wanted. You have more covers to design. So Get Ready Girl! ☺

Mr. Luni Films where do I begin? Thank you for gambling on me. I appreciate you seeing my vision and executing it beyond my imagination. Your time, patience, & positive energy was greatly appreciated. & the magic you put into making the mini movie for "Refuse to Lose Faith" & "Finding Faith" is indescribable. Working with you was an amazing experience & I pray we can work on a bigger project in the future.

To everyone that took time out their day to read my books, send encouraging words, follow me on social media, donate to my nonprofit "Purple Diamonds Inc.," or visited my website. I thank you.

Your Support Is Greatly Appreciated.

TO THE BEST GRANDMA IN THE WORLD

Dear Grandma,

It's impossible to put into words everything that I love and appreciate about you, because everything about you is amazing. So I wrote you this poem.

Grandma you mean the world to me,

Only a heart as pure as yours can love unselfishly,

No matter what you're always there,

Giving tough love, while showing you care.

You are my cushion when I fall,

And my voice of reason when I call,

You were my eyes when I couldn't see,

And you always saw the best in me.

You were my shelter when I needed to escape,

And proof that not all Super Heroes wear capes.

You are my sun, my moon, and all my stars,

Thank you for everything that you are.

 *I LOVE YOU GRANDMA A.K.A. GRANNY G*

CONTENTS

DIFFERENT TEACHER; SAME PROBLEM

I thought things would be different since I transitioned to eighth grade, boy was I wrong.

One Friday afternoon while we were taking a test, (*When we take exams, the class is quiet. If you talk during testing, Ms. Perkins takes your test and gives you an F.*)

I heard my classmates whispering.

I looked around the classroom to see what was going on. That's when I saw some of them pointing at the door. So, I looked in the direction of their points.

"Oh My God!" I gasped in disbelief and instantly became sick to my stomach.

My heart began beating extremely fast and I could barely hold my pencil because I was shaking so much.

"Isn't that your daddy Destiny?" One of my classmates asked.

I was motionless and mute. Ms. Perkins was calling my name but I couldn't answer. I didn't intentionally disrespect her, it was just that his presents frightened me, and fear had taking over my body.

"Settle down class and continue taking your test," Ms. Perkins said before she left out the room to talk to that M.A.N.

Unexpectedly one of my classmates asked, "Destiny who did you lie on this time?"

Another classmate replied, "It better not be me, because I will beat your ass and I don't give a fuck who you tell!"

The entire class laughed.

I tried to ignore them, but their words and laugher made it difficult to do so.

However, they were the least of my worries; because my focus was on that M.A.N.'s intentions.

Ms. Perkins opened the door and called me into the hall.

As I exited the classroom, all my classmates were laughing and whispering, so Ms. Perkins closed the door.

Both she and that M.A.N. looked at me silently.

That M.A.N.'s arms were folded, he had a frown on his face, and rage was in his eyes.

I looked at the floor to avoid all eye contact with him.

"Your teacher tells me you like talking to yourself when class is in session!" He yelled.

I looked at Ms. Perkins as she clarified her statement.

"I explained to your father that you are a very good student, but sometimes you talk to yourself. I also told him that I think something is bothering you from your actions alone. Because right before Christmas break, I thought you were crying. Is there something bothering you?"

I shook my head, because that woman had no idea that her words just signed my death certificate.

That M.A.N. never took those demonic eyes off me, nor did he take that frown off his face.

"So what's your problem?" He shouted.

Before I could answer, he smacked me.

He smacked me so hard that my classmates heard it, and the classroom door was closed.

I didn't cry because I was too embarrassed.

I went back into the classroom stumping and mumbling. Trying to act as if I was madder than I really was. That way my classmates wouldn't know that M.A.N. smacked me. But neither my stumps nor mumbles could conceal the truth.

Everyone was staring at me, waiting for a reaction, but I didn't give them one.

The class was silent for about 90 seconds. Then a classmate broke the silence by asking, "Destiny did your daddy smack you?"

"No," I answered.

Another classmate said, "Destiny you know damn well he smacked the fuck out your ass. You can't deny it, we heard that shit."

Everyone laughed.

Then another classmate asked, "Why do your daddy abuse you?"

That comment tickled them pink, because their laughs got even louder.

I was so broken, mad, sad, and embarrassed by that M.A.N.'s actions and my classmates' words.

And although tears weren't exiting my eyes, my soul was crying.

Experiencing all those emotions at once made my heart tired. I acted as if I was unbothered, but inside it was killing me. I just wanted to cry and scream and let all the pain out.

I was hurt, humiliated, upset, ashamed, and afraid. I wanted to tell someone what that M.A.N. was doing to me, but who could I trust?

I was exhausted from trying to be stronger than I felt.

The tears had become too hard to hold back.

However, I didn't want to cry because I didn't want to feel weak and vulnerable.

But I had been strong for too long, and my eyes felt like a balloon with too much air.

I was about to emotionally explode and there wasn't anything I could do about it.

When that M.A.N. left, Ms. Perkins returned to class. She then said, "Settle down class."

However, they continued with the insults, jokes, and negative comments.

I wanted to run and hide, but I had nowhere to go. I needed to conceal my pain and I needed to do it quickly, because internalizing my tears was drowning my heart. And I was about to emotionally breakdown because my heart was struggling to breathe.

At that moment, I remembered something I read by Maya Angelou, ***"there is no greater agony than bearing an untold story inside of you."***

Her words gave me the courage to let my tongue speak what my heart was feeling. But before I had a chance to collect my thoughts, tears fell from my eyes as pain poured from my heart.

So, I began telling my painful truth in a form of a poem. A poem that rolled off my tongue as if it was prewritten.

"Everyone thinks I'm wrong, never questioning why I don't want to go home, and although I try to stay strong, my heart is bleeding

cause I'm all alone. I cry but my tears are ignored, I pray to God, but where is my Lord? I'm tired, hurt, and frustrated, feeling separated and dissociated. Faking a smile pretending to be fine, losing my mind, haven't slept in a long time. Afraid that one day I'm going to flat line, because my mom is blind, acting like everything is fine.

But it's not; and I'm hurting a lot, reflecting on my life, I'm all I got. I get smack, teachers turn their backs, closing their eyes and ignoring the facts, ignoring my cries, believing the lies, acting like they don't see the tears that fall from my eyes?

Classmates find humor in my pain, thinking that abuse is a game, and I am emotionally drained, I just want to put a bullet in my brain.

The cruel things people say and do, only makes me more miserable, and I am not invisible, so it's easy to see what I'm going through.

Heavenly Father Are You Near? Can You hear, my every tear, that falls from my eyes, because You don't verbalize, whether or not You hear my cries. Are they in vain? Because I'm in pain, Lord I'm in so much pain, too weak to maintain, I'm going insane.

And if this is a test, God I must confess, it's best, if You just lay me to rest. Cause my life is hard, I'm falling apart, and I'm mentally and emotionally scarred.

And since no one cares what happens to me, let me be, so I can be free, cause it's not difficult to see, what this M.A.N. is doing to me. And if you pay attention you'll see the proof, but no one wants to believe the truth, cause he's a reverend and I'm a

youth.

So don't inquire, when I expire, cause y'all

had the chance to stop this fire. But no one did,

they ignored this kid, and now the abuse is forever

hid. And since you want to believe the lies, I'm going

to say my last goodbyes, so for everyone that ignored

my cries, don't act surprised, when you realize, that

sanctified loving father act, is just a disguise."

I put my head on my desk and cried as if I was in

the room all alone. I cried so hard that I was gasping to

catch my breath. My nose was running, and I couldn't stop

sniffing. I was trembling as if I was cold, but I was

sweating as if I was hot. I was so mad at myself for being a

coward. I was mad at mom, Tish, Mel, Stanley, Kenya,

Ms. Perkins, and my daddy. I was really mad at my daddy

for not sticking around and protecting me.

I hated him more than I hated that M.A.N. because he should have been there to give me the love I desired. If I wasn't searching for a father, to seal the hole he left in my heart, the day he went incognito, that M.A.N. would've never had the opportunity to manipulate me.

I was afraid because I knew what was at home waiting for me. And I was depressed because no one would save me. I continued to cry hysterically. At that moment, I didn't care if my classmates laughed or criticized me, because I needed to release those emotions.

Ms. Perkins looked at me as if she wanted to cry. She wondered if she made the right decision when she spoke with that M.A.N.

Whatever, she was feeling; she didn't express it to me. And obviously she didn't express her feelings to the proper authorities either. Because nothing in my life changed for the better, only for the worse.

When I got home, that M.A.N. took me to the basement and beat me. Then had sex with me and made me take a shower. Yep that was my life, and what a sad life it was.

DYING TO PLEASE

I thought about my biological father quite often. Although I never met him, I was convinced he would save me.

He would physically demolish that M.A.N., then take me away with him. Away from the pain, the misery, and the torture.

My daddy was going to rescue me. I was sure of it; I was just waiting for that day to come.

Every Father's Day I made him a card, dated it, and kept it under my mattress.

Although I never seen my daddy's face, heard his voice, or felt his touch, I still loved him, because I was a part of him, and he was a part of me.

For several weeks, mom complained about migraine headaches. It had gotten so bad that one day she had to leave work to go to the hospital.

During her visit, the doctor diagnosed her with depression.

He prescribed her Zoloft and placed her on bedrest for a week.

Sadly, after two days, that M.A.N. persuaded mom to go back to work.

He promised her that she wouldn't have to work much longer, because he was going to have a church soon and they will be set for life.

And because she lived to please her husband, she returned to work.

One evening while mom was at work she fainted. She was rushed to the hospital.

Her depression had gotten so severe that it caused her to be hospitalized for a week.

The doctor explained that her depression was triggered by stress, but lack of sleep caused her body to shut down. So he prescribed her something to help her sleep.

Mom was killing herself trying to keep her husband happy and her struggling life a secret.

She put her foot in her mouth when she boasted about how great her life was, and accused grandma, Aunt Jasmine, and my uncles of envying her and that M.A.N.

She also told grandma that she would never ever ask her for anything again, and because of that, she had to work even harder to disguise her truth.

While mom was in the hospital that M.A.N. was at home having sex with me.

He would visit mom while I was in school, but leave when I was dismissed. His excuse for leaving was, he needed to work on his sermon for the week. But what he was really working on, was me.

He molested and raped me from the time I got home from school, until the time Kenya got in from practice.

That Friday Kenya was cheering at a basketball game and didn't return home until after nine o'clock.

Stanley spent the night with his buddy, so he didn't come home at all.

And since mom was in the hospital, there was no one to stop that M.A.N.'s evil hands from touching me, and his rotten penis from internally damaging me.

I endured hours of sexual abuse.

Minute after minute and hour after hour, he violated me.

My body was sore, my heart was wounded, and my soul was crushed.

That M.A.N. treated me like his personal prostitute and I was too weak to stop him.

My life was not my life, and my body was not my body.

When he beat, raped, and molested me in the past, I was hurt but I still found enough strength to carry on.

But, that day was different from all the rest.

I couldn't sleep, cause every time I closed my eyes, the memories of that M.A.N.'s evil body parts violating me played in my head. I couldn't stop crying and shaking.

I just wanted my mind to erase the horrible memories.

I wish I could have sanitized my brain, then maybe, just maybe, I would feel a little better.

But no matter how hard I tried, I could not comprehend why God allowed something so horrific to happen to me.

All the unanswered questions, terrible memories, and self-guilt became too much to handle.

I was sad, angry, confused, ashamed, scared, depressed, but mostly broken.

I was mad at everyone including myself.

I blamed mom for being in the hospital, I blamed Stanley for staying the night at his buddy's house, I blamed Kenya for going to that basketball game, I blamed my biological daddy for not saving me, I blamed Tish and Mel for moving out, I blamed grandma for not being there like she promised, I blamed Aunt Jasmine for not defending me when mom said I couldn't go to her house for Christmas Break, I blamed Ms. Perkins for not calling the police, I blamed God for putting that M.A.N. in my life, and I blamed myself for not having enough courage to stop him.

NO MORE PAIN

Mom and that M.A.N. decided that Kenya and I were getting older and needed our individual privacy. So they moved Kenya into Tish's old bedroom.

When I was younger, I played with all the children in my neighborhood. We jumped rope, played basketball with a milk crate we cut the bottom out of and hung up on a light pole, hopscotch, hide-and-seek, tag, if you step on a crack you break your mama's back, jacks, and baseball with a large stick and a tennis ball.

I used to have so much fun, but once that M.A.N. started abusing me, I was no longer allowed to go outside.

A lot of new children moved into the neighborhood, but I didn't know any of them. The only people I knew my age were Myeisha and Pam, and that's because we played together when I was allowed to go out.

Pam went to a different school because she was two years older than I was.

And although Myeisha and I were the same age, we attended different schools as well.

Myeisha went to private school from kindergarten to seventh grade. But when she got to eighth grade she begged her father to transfer her to public school, and since she was a daddy's girl, he did it.

Fortunately for me, her daddy transferred her to the school I attended.

Myeisha and I became good friends because we walked to and from school together.

Our daily conversations allowed us to become really close.

She told me secrets that I swore to never tell anyone and I told her lies because my real life sucked.

Besides I only had one secret and if I revealed that secret it could possibly cost me my friendship.

Myeisha and I weren't in the same class, but we ate lunch together every day. And our walks to and from school helped me keep my mind off the abuse momentarily.

Myeisha and I talked daily, and no matter what we talked about she always incorporated her daddy in our conversations.

She loved him so much and she was so blessed to have a daddy that genuinely loved her.

She was the only child so she didn't have to share her parents love and attention with anyone.

Her parents were high school sweet hearts. Her mother was a stay at home mom and her father was the Chief Technology Officer (CTO) at a very popular computer company.

One day Ms. Perkins handed out flyers inviting us to the school's Valentine's Day dance. I really wanted to go. However, I didn't have any money or anything to wear.

On our way home from school Myeisha said, "my daddy is taking me shopping Saturday. He's going to buy me a purse with matching shoes."

I was quiet because I was secretly jealous. Not because she was getting new shoes and a purse, but because she had a great father. And a great father was something I yearned for.

I just didn't understand my life. Why did my siblings have daddies? Yet I was fatherless. Even if their dads weren't the best, at least they knew them. I didn't know anything about my daddy. I didn't even know his name.

I often wondered, *do I favor him? Do I have aunts and uncles? Do I have grandparents? Does he have other children?*

I was so busy daydreaming about my daddy that I didn't hear Myeisha calling my name.

"Earth to Destiny," she said while snapping her fingers.

"Huh?" I answered.

"Do you want to go shopping with us Saturday?"

"No, I'm on punishment."

"Again? What did you do this time?" She asked.

"I don't know?"

"Wait, so you're not going to the dance?"

"Unfortunately, not."

"Why not?"

"Because I don't have anything to wear."

"Girl that's it? You can borrow something from my closet," she said.

"I can?" I asked shockingly.

"Sure you can. Come over anytime."

"What about now? Can I come over now?"

"Sure," she replied.

So instead of going home, I went to Myeisha's house.

Their house was so beautiful. Myeisha had her own bathroom, a canopy bed, and a walk in closet full of shoes, clothes, and purses.

On her dresser was a customized jewelry box with her name printed on the top. When it opened, a ballerina danced, as "The Nutcracker" played. And on her nightstand was a picture of her parents.

"Are you ready to play dress up?" Myeisha asked.

I didn't reply because I didn't want to seem anxious and needy. But inside my heart was dancing.

Myeisha and I picked out what I was going to wear to the dance. Although I had the perfect outfit, I still didn't have the four dollars needed to attend.

In the midst of me trying on outfits I thought about that M.A.N. and how much trouble I was going to be in when I got home.

I looked out of Myeisha's bedroom window and when I saw the van parked in front of our house, I shook my head because that M.A.N. hadn't left to pick mom up from work yet.

I debated should I go home, and decided not to, because if I did he was going to beat and sexually abuse me.

I knew there would be a beating waiting for me whenever I returned home, but I would cross that bridge when the time was necessary.

Myeisha and I talked, watched television, and ate sandwiches and chips.

I was planning to go home after that M.A.N. picked mom up from work but I lost track of time. When I realized how late it was, I left.

I mentally prepared myself for the beating I was about to receive. So I took a deep breath before I put the key in the door. As soon as I opened it, that M.A.N. was

standing in the living room holding that thick wooden stick.

"Where have you been?" He asked.

"I don't know," I answered.

"You don't know?" He repeated.

I didn't answer I just stood there fearlessly waiting

for my beating.

"Do your mom know where you were?"

"I don't know," I replied.

"Do you think I'm playing with you?"

"I don't know."

That M.A.N. began swinging that stick with anger

and hostility, hitting me any and everywhere he could. I

covered my face with my hands, fell to the floor and bald

up in a fetal position, as he continued aggressively

swinging.

Then the stick broke.

When I realized he stopped hitting me, I slowly removed my hands and looked at him.

As he attempted to fix the stick, I quickly got up from the floor, ran to my bedroom, and locked the door.

He yelled and screamed while banging on my room door, but I refused to open it.

Instead I turned my radio up as loud as it would go, sat on the floor holding my knees against my chest, rocking back and forth, and crying.

I was so scared.

At that moment Mary J. Blige song came on the radio and I began singing to help calm my mind and heart.

"I don't know, only God knows where the story ends for me.

But I know where the story begins. It's up to me to choose, whether I win or lose.

And I choose to win.

No more pain, No more pain, No more

pain

No more drama in my life

No one's gonna make me hurt again.

No more tears, No more crying every

night.

No more waking me up in the morning,

telling me to make your coffee.

Leave me alone Chris, go to hell. Yeah,

Yeah!"

VALENTINE'S DAY

It was Tuesday February 14th and I woke up later than usual.

Once I realized how late it was, I moved as fast as I could because I knew that M.A.N. would use that as an excuse to chastise me when I got home.

I quickly got ready, put my backpack at the front door, prepared their coffee, and took it to them.

When I got to their bedroom mom and that M.A.N. were both in the bathroom.

When I sat the cups of coffee on their dresser, I noticed mom's purse. I tipped toed to the door to make sure no one was coming. My heart was beating a hundred miles an hour because I was terrified. But I really wanted to go to the Valentine's Day dance.

So I quickly unzipped her purse, grabbed a five-dollar bill, zipped it closed, ran out their bedroom, grabbed my backpack, and flew out the front door.

But once I opened the door, Myeisha was standing in the doorway about to knock. In her hand was the outfit she was letting me borrow.

"Girl what are you doing?" I asked.

"Are you still going to the dance?"

"Yes, but I'm not getting dressed here."

"Well, I assumed you wanted me to meet you here because you're usually at my house by this time."

"I woke up late, now let's go!" I said as I snatched her by the arm.

When we got to Myeisha's house, I went in her bathroom and got dressed.

As I was getting ready, Myeisha walked in with her jewelry box. She dropped it when she saw me half naked.

"What happened to you?" She screamed.

"Why didn't you knock?" I yelled as I quickly slammed the bathroom door.

I was so embarrassed.

When I was done getting dressed, I helped Myeisha pick her jewelry up.

"Sorry I slammed the door in your face, but you should've knocked."

"What happened to you?" Myeisha inquired.

"I don't want to talk about it."

Although Myeisha didn't question me anymore, I knew her well enough to know that she was too nosey to let it go.

"Let me do your hair," she said changing the subject.

She grabbed her comb and brush and began styling my hair.

"I don't remember your hair being this thin," she mumbled.

Myeisha added extensions to my hair, neatly braided the top, and crinkled the back to help blend my natural hair with the hair weave.

Myeisha wanted to be a beautician and own her own shop when she grew up. I believed she had the potential to do so, because she was really good at styling hair. She didn't just style my hair, she also styled her mother's, grandmother's, aunts', cousins', and other girls in the neighborhood hair as well.

I never thought about what I wanted to be when I grew up. Because I never thought that far ahead. My goal was to get through my todays so that I could experience my tomorrows.

School ended early due to the Valentine's Day Dance. The dance was at noon and ended at four o'clock. I really enjoyed myself.

After the dance Myeisha and I walked home. I knew I was going to be in trouble, but it didn't matter because I had fun. Besides I was always in trouble, whether I did something or not.

As we walked home Myeisha stared at me silently.

"What's the matter with you?" I asked while smirking.

"How did you get those bruises on your body?"

My smirk quickly turned into a frown and I suddenly changed the subject.

"Today is my biological daddy's birthday, I have to make him a card when I get home," I lied.

"Do not change the subject Destiny. What happened to you?"

"Why can't you just let it go?" I yelled.

"Because I'm your friend!" She shouted.

"Okay real friends leave you alone!" I screamed.

"No, they help you!" Myeisha cried.

Her words soothed my heart. So, I replied, "If I tell you what happened, you have to promise not to tell anyone."

"I promise," Myeisha replied as she raised her right hand.

She stared at me anxiously waiting for an answer, but I was too ashamed to say anything. Suddenly she asked, "did that M.A.N. do that to you? Did he?"

A tear fell from my eye as I nodded my head.

"I hate him! Why did he do that to you? That bastard!" Myeisha yelled.

Myeisha asked me other questions, but I didn't answer because it was too difficult to talk about. When she saw the pain in my eyes she just wrapped her arms around me and said, "it's okay friend. Your secret is safe with me."

Instead of going straight home, I went to Myeisha's house to change into my original clothes.

When I got home, that M.A.N. was sitting on the couch waiting for me.

"Where have you been? And you better not say I don't know!"

"I was at school."

"No, you were not!"

"Yes, I was."

"No, you weren't!"

"Alright then," I said as I shrugged my shoulders.

"So, where were you?"

I stood there silently waiting for that M.A.N. to make his next move.

"You quiet because you're lying!" He yelled.

"I'm not lying. I'm silent because the truth does not need defending."

"Your ass is going to need defending in a minute, now, where were you?"

"Okay since you know where I wasn't, then tell me where I was," I replied courageously.

That M.A.N. smacked me so hard that I saw a flash of light. He then pushed me against the wall and started choking me.

"Please stop!" I cried as I tried to escape his grip.

He threw me on the floor by my neck.

"Where did you get money from?" He shouted while standing over me.

"I don't have any money!" I cried assuming he found out about the money I stole from mom's purse earlier.

"How did you get your hair done?"

"Myeisha did it for me."

"Do I have dumb written across my forehead?" *It needs to be along with the words pedophile, phony, and uneducated.* "I know your ass was somewhere getting your hair done! Who are you trying to look good for? Those little nappy head boys you let touch you?"

Unexpectedly I shouted, "I don't, nor have I ever, allow boys to touch me! You are the only one that touches me inappropriately! You asked me did I allow boys to touch me, and I told you no, but you beat me until I told you what you wanted to hear. And then you went to my school and made me lie on two of my classmates!"

I knew he was about to hit me, because the look in his eyes were full of rage. But he didn't just hit me, he turned psychotic. He kicked and punched me while calling me names. I bald up into a fetal position and covered my face.

"Who the fuck do you think you're talking to? You're a fucking whore! A dirty dumb ass whore!" He yelled as he continued abusing me.

When he stopped, I slowly uncovered my face to see where he went. When I tried to get up from the floor, he spit in my face. I angrily wiped off the saliva.

"Get up and go put on your pajamas!" He demanded.

I wanted to protect myself, but I was too weak and too afraid. Besides I was home alone with him, so I did as I was told.

After I put on my pajamas he molested me, then bent me over and had sex with me.

As usual when he was done he made me take a shower. After my shower, he took me to the basement and beat me. And when he was done beating me, he molested me again. Once he untied me, he ordered me to clean the house.

When I was done cleaning, I went to my bedroom to do my homework. But on my way down the stairs he called my name. *What more could he possibly want?*

When I got to his bedroom he asked me, "did you do what I told you to do?"

"Yes sir," I replied.

He took me around the house and inspected every room to make sure I cleaned everything properly. Although he could not find one mistake, he still smacked me.

I didn't understand why he slapped me; but it's a lot of things I didn't understand about that M.A.N.

When I didn't show any emotions, he took the back of his hand and slapped me again. I held my face as it stung with pain. I was afraid, angry, and frustrated. But despite all those emotions I was feeling, I refused to cry.

He stared at me as if he was waiting for a reaction. I tried my best not to allow my fear to be visible, because I knew he preyed on me being afraid of him. He gazed at me silently with those demonic eyes. I felt like an animal being taken by its predator.

I don't know what came over me, but I mimicked him by returning the stares. We stood there momentarily having a staring contest, and with no warning at all, he walked away and left out the front door.

I was speechless; and clueless as to what happened.

I went to my bedroom, closed my door, locked it, and got my journal from under my mattress.

While I was writing, I heard someone twist the door knob.

When they realized my door was locked, they began beating on it like a psychopath. By that time, I knew it was that M.A.N. So, I put my journal under my mattress and unlocked the door.

That M.A.N. did not give me a chance to let him in; he just burst into my bedroom.

When he swung the door open, I fell to the floor.

"Why did you lock the door?" He yelled.

"I thought you left to pick mom up from work."

"Don't lock this door. You don't pay any bills in this house."

Hell, you don't either. All you do is eat, sleep, smoke cigarettes, abuse me, and make demands.

"I'm on my way to pick your mother up from work," he stated as if I cared.

Shortly after he left to pick mom up from work, Pam knocked on the front door.

"Hey Destiny."

"What's up Pam."

"I am going to pick up my Valentine's Day gift from my boyfriend, but I don't want to go alone, will you go with me?" She asked.

At first, I told her, I couldn't because I had homework to do, but she promised me she'll be quick, so I agreed to go.

When we got to Pam's boyfriend's house, he did not have a gift for her. She was very upset, so I told her, "Let's go!"

But he wanted to explain, and she wanted to listen.

Pam begged me to stay so she could hear his sorry excuses. I knew I should've left, but I didn't. I honestly don't know why I didn't leave. I guess I was like that caged animal that was finally free. And I wasn't in a rush to go back to my cage.

It was getting late and time was passing rapidly. I had to get home before mom and that M.A.N., otherwise I was going to be in big trouble.

But like a dummy I stood there waiting for Pam to finish talking and kissing her boyfriend.

"What time is it?" I asked.

Pam's boyfriend looked at his watch and said, "its five minutes to seven."

My heart sunk to the pit of my stomach because mom and that M.A.N. were usually home at that time. But I was hoping they stopped at the store before returning home.

"Come on Pam, I have to go!"

Pam had no intentions on leaving, so I waved my hand and began walking home. Once she realized I left, she began to follow. By the time I got close enough to see my house… **"DAMN!"** The family van was parked in front.

So many thoughts crossed my mind. *What was I going to do? Did they notice I was gone? Could I sneak in and pretend I was asleep?*

Pam went home, and I went to my back door. I was hoping that M.A.N. and mom didn't notice I was gone, that way I could sneak in and pretend I've been home the entire time.

I went in my pocket to get my keys. When I checked my right pocket, the keys were not there. So, I checked my left pocket, still no keys. I checked my back pockets, then my coat pockets. I checked all my pockets once more. ***Oh My God! I left my keys in the house!***

Once I realized I didn't have my keys, I ran down the street to Pam's house to use her telephone. I was hoping Stanley, Kenya, or mom would answer, that way they could help me sneak in the house.

But when I knocked on Pam's door, her mother came out the house aggressively screaming, "why are you here? You need to go home. Your parents are worried about you, and your father is looking for you!"

Oh My Lord! He knows I'm gone!

On my way home, I ran into Myeisha. I did not acknowledge her right away because I was still processing the information I received from Pam's mother.

"Destiny have you been home yet?" She asked.

I shook my head.

"Do you know that M.A.N. was walking around the neighborhood with an extension cord looking for you?"

My mouth dropped, because I was thunderstruck.

"An extension cord?" I asked shockingly.

"Yep, he knocked on my door and asked my parents were you here. And when they told him no, he told my parents that you were on punishment and wasn't supposed to leave the house. And because you were being disobedient he's going to embarrass you by whipping you in public.

My daddy told him not to do that because that will follow you for the rest of your life, and when it comes to physically disciplining a daughter, its best to let the mother do it.

But that M.A.N.'s only response was, "**Proverbs 23:34 –** Whoever spares the rod hates his son, but he who loves him is diligent to discipline him."

That M.A.N.'s comment irritated my daddy, and my daddy replied, "right son, not daughter. And any mother that allows her husband to whip her daughter is no woman at all! And any man that embarrasses their child in public is not a man."

That M.A.N. told my daddy that, "your opinion is just that, yours."

My daddy then replied, "it's not my opinion, its fucking abuse and your daughter is going to grow up despising you."

That M.A.N.'s only reply was, "**Proverbs 22:6 – Train up a child in the way he should go; even when he is old he will not depart from it.**"

That M.A.N. upset my daddy so bad that my daddy replied, "what does the bible say about child abuse?"

Then my mom intervened and told my daddy to stop being mean, so my daddy shook his head and went in the house. So that M.A.N. phoniness didn't fool my daddy, but my mom on the other hand sat outside and talked to that M.A.N. for over thirty minutes. They were laughing and giggling, as if you being whipped in public was something to joke about."

Tears silently trickled down my cheeks because I didn't think the situation was that serious. I would've never imagined that he would walk around the neighborhood looking for me with an extension cord in hand. Thank God he didn't see me, because I would've been humiliated.

What I couldn't understand was, if my whereabouts was such a concern, then why was he looking for me and not mom? And I agree with Mr. Jones, why would mom allow him to embarrass me in public?

"Do you want me to call the police and report the abuse?" Myeisha asked.

I didn't answer her, because I was still in shock.

I wanted someone to protect me, but my mind was so cluttered. I didn't know if I was coming or going, because fear had me in a chokehold.

Myeisha gave me a quick hug, then went back into her house.

I slowly walked home to face my punishment.

I took a deep breath and softly knocked on the back door.

I prayed that Stanley or Kenya would open it.

My heart was thumping because I didn't know what to expect.

The door swiftly swung open and various parts of my body was stinging with pain. After a few seconds, I realized that M.A.N. was hitting me with an extension cord.

My legs, thighs, stomach, arms, face, back; he hit me any and everywhere, with no remorse. So, I put my arms up to protect my face.

"Go take your coat off and meet me in the basement!" He demanded.

Instead of taking my coat off. I ran up the stairs to mom's bedroom. Mom was lying in bed, watching television, and eating leftover lasagna. My heart was beating fast, my mind was spinning, and words were exiting my mouth rapidly.

Mom put her plate on the nightstand and sat up in her bed.

"Slow down," she said, as if she cared to listen.

I took a deep breath and began explaining a little slower.

"Every day while you're at work your husband molests me."

Mom looked at me and asked, "Molests you how?"

"He rubs my breast and put his finger and penis in my vagina."

At that moment, that M.A.N. walked into the bedroom with the extension cord still in his hand.

Mom looked at him and said, "Destiny said you molested her."

That M.A.N. looked at me with those evil eyes and denied everything. All the fear I felt had suddenly disappeared, because I knew mom would protect me.

I snatched the extension cord out of his hand and said, "Mom when you were in the hospital he repeatedly raped me. That was the worst week of my life, because no one was there to stop him.

And every day I come home from school he has sex with me and then beat me. He raped me today mom!"

That M.A.N. looked at mom and said, "I swear to God I never touched her."

Mom looked at him and then looked at me. She looked at him once more and replied, "I don't know who to believe."

Her words knocked the air out of my lungs. It felt like I've been stabbed in the heart with a machete.

I could not believe she allowed those words to exit her mouth. Even if she thought it, why did she have to verbalize it? I was upset, sad, and hurt. I raised my shirt and pulled down my pants.

"Look At This! Do It Look Like I'm Lying!" I yelled, exposing both old and new bruises. "Why do you think he beats me so much? He does it, so I would fear him!"

Mom wasn't convinced so I yelled, "take me to the doctor."

"What is that going to prove?" That M.A.N. asked quickly.

"It's going to support the truth," I screamed.

"What truth? That you're sexually active? We already know that you allow boys to touch you. There's no telling what else you allow them to do to you."

"So I let them put these bruises on me?" I yelled.

I looked at mom's blank facial expression and I could see she was persuaded by that M.A.N.'s lies, so I immediately shouted, **"Ask Kenya!"**

When mom turned to put her slippers on, that M.A.N. mumbled, "I knew you were about to tell on me."

I looked at mom to see if she heard him, but obviously she didn't, because she left her bedroom and closed the door behind her.

What the hell was she thinking? Did she not hear me tell her this M.A.N. molested and beat me? Why would she leave me in the room with him? And why would she close the door?

I tried to leave out behind her, but when I got up, that M.A.N. grabbed me by the back of my neck, pulled me back down to the bed, and said, "You better not tell her I put my penis in you."

All of the fear returned and my body was shaking uncontrollably, because I realized mom was not going to protect me.

Mom returned to her bedroom and said, "Kenya admit she witnessed you touching Destiny."

Oh my God now he is going to kill both Kenya and me.

He looked at mom, and when he realized the truth had been revealed, he put his head down and said, "I did it baby, I touched her once or twice, and I am so sorry."

At that moment, I was over the bullshit.

A sudden dose of courage filled my body. I stood there stern and brave, as I yelled, "it was more than once or twice. You been sexually abusing me for damn near two years. Tell the truth Reverend! Tell your wife how you forced your penis in me multiple times and how you make me shower after you ejaculate inside of me. You often preach about how the truth will set you free, well I hope the truth lock your ass up!"

That M.A.N. continued to let those phony tears fall. Mom looked at me, then she looked at him and said, "we went through this with Tish and you promised it would never happen again."

I could not believe my ears. He was supposed to be out of our lives a long time ago.

That M.A.N. replied, "I never put my penis in Tish.

I touched Destiny, and I was wrong baby. God can fix this baby. Let's pray about it. A family that prays together, stays together."

Tears fell from mom's eyes, and then the unimaginable happened. She grabbed that M.A.N. and pulled him towards her. He laid on her chest as she consoled him. "It will be alright! We will get through this together," she said while she gently caressed his head.

I gazed at mom in disbelief.

When she noticed I was staring at her with wet eyes, she said, "meet me in the family room."

I was flabbergasted and speechless. My mind was boggled. All I could do was stare at her as tears fell from my eyes, hurt poured from my heart, confusion leaked from my brain, and my soul wept in agony.

Why was she so blind? How could she not see that that M.A.N. was not a victim, he was an abuser?

That pervert didn't need my mother, I needed my mother. I needed her love and protection. I needed her to embrace me, hold me, and console me.

Sadly, I stood there hopelessly waiting for something that would never happen.

When I walked away I didn't go into the family room; instead I went to my bedroom, locked my door, and pulled out my journal.

My mind was so discombobulated.

I was physically, mentally, emotionally, and spiritually drained.

I wanted to write, but I couldn't collect my thoughts. Things I wanted to write down, only made me cry more. My tears dripped onto the empty pages.

So many emotions were flowing through my body. I was crying angry tears, sad tears, scared tears, hurtful tears, ashamed tears, worthless tears, hopeless tears, betrayed tears, and tears that I could not identify.

I was so broken. I was so weak. And I was so tired.

My mind and heart could not process mom's reaction. How could she console him and not me? Especially after he admitted to sexually abusing me?

Grandma said, "people will admit what they can't deny, and deny what they can't admit."

That M.A.N. could no longer deny touching me once mom asked Kenya. So he admitted to molesting me, but denied having sex with me, because that was something he wasn't willing to confess.

But even if he had; what would've changed? Not a damn thing, because it was obvious that mom wasn't going to divorce that fool.

All my thoughts only made my heart break more. I needed to write because writing was my coping mechanism. I dated the top of the damp paper.

Then I wrote,

Dear Heavenly Father,

Please hear my tears as they fall from my eyes onto this paper, because they speak louder than any words I could write or say. My soul is broken and my heart is shattered.

The words I want to write, can't be expressed. And the feelings that I feel can't be explained. Why try anyway? Not like anyone is concern with my wellbeing, my happiness, or my safety.

Heavenly Father my voice has been silenced, my tears have gone unnoticed, and my bruises has been overlooked.

So, I cry. I cry because I'm lonely, I cry because I'm scared, I cry because I'm hurting, I cry because I'm embarrassed, I cry because I've been violated, I cry because my self-esteem is low, I cry because I've been betrayed, I cry because I am lacking confidence, I cry because I'm angry, I cry for my daddy, I cry for my mommy, I cry for help, I cry for You Lord, I cry for hope, I cry for faith, I cry so much that sometimes I forget what I'm crying about. And since my cries have gone unheard and my tears disregarded, I am just going to let them flow. Maybe if I allow my feelings to drip onto this paper, my pain will finally be acknowledged.

I put my journal under my mattress and grabbed a jigsaw puzzle off the dresser, in hopes that it would take my mind off the hurtful situation.

While I was figuring out how to organize two hundred puzzle pieces, I began humming, *""it's me, it's me, it's me oh Lord, standing in the need of prayer…. it's me, it's me, it's me oh Lord, standing in the need of prayer…not my father, not my mother…but it's me oh Lord, standing in the need of prayer…. not my sister not my brother…but it's me oh Lord standing in the need of prayer…."*

While I was working and humming someone knocked on my bedroom door.

I didn't want to be bothered, I just wanted to be left alone. But when I ignored the person on the other end of the door, they continued knocking.

So I unlocked it, and went back to doing my puzzle.

The door knob turned and the door slowly opened.

It was mom and she invited herself into my bedroom.

I ignored her and continued humming while organizing the puzzle pieces.

"Your grandmother used to sing that song," she said.

I stopped humming and continued working quietly.

Mom sat on my bed and silently watched me put together the puzzle. After about two minutes she said, "for now on, pick Kenya up from school and you guys come home together."

I stopped putting the puzzle together and cut my eyes at her.

"What will Kenya do if he tries to kill me?"

"He's not going to kill you Destiny?"

"Are you going to call the police or put him out?"

Mom didn't reply.

"So you're just going to ignore my questions?" I asked.

She remained speechless.

I stared at her quietly waiting for her to show me some type of affection.

Although I wasn't crying I knew she saw the pain in my eyes, but instead of comforting me, she replied, "don't forget to wash the dishes."

She then left and went upstairs with her phony, hypocritical, child molesting husband.

When mom went upstairs, I went to the kitchen to wash the dishes.

I don't know what came over me, but unexpectedly tears fell from my eyes.

"Fuck This Shit!!!" I yelled as I began throwing dishes against the wall.

The sound of glass breaking caught the attention of Stanley, Kenya, mom, and that M.A.N.

They all ran to the kitchen to see what all the commotion was.

"Destiny what the hell are you doing?" Mom shouted.

"Fuck these bitch ass dishes!" I yelled.

That M.A.N. looked at me as if he wanted to say something.

I grabbed a butcher knife, stabbed the counter, and yelled, "What?"

Mom looked at her husband and calmly said, "Just give her some space."

"Destiny!" Stanley yelled.

"Stanley why the fuck are you calling my name? And what the fuck are you doing here? Didn't your ass move out or some shit?"

Stanley, Kenya, that M.A.N., and mom all stood there silently, as I continued crying and throwing dishes against the wall.

That M.A.N. was the first to walk away and the rest of them followed.

I went into my bedroom, locked the door, fell to the floor, and cried like never before.

I didn't understand what was wrong with my mother? She didn't drink, didn't do drugs, and she did not fear him. So what could it be? Is she really that in love with him that she would choose him over her own children?

That night I barely slept because I was worried about that M.A.N. entering my bedroom. Although my door was locked, I didn't feel safe.

My heart was emotionally aching. I was tired…tired of my classmates, tired of that M.A.N., tired of mom, tired of my siblings, tired of the abuse, tired of being afraid, tired of feeling helpless, and tired of living.

I got out of bed, went to the bathroom, and looked in the medicine cabinet. As soon as I opened the cabinet door, mom's bottle of Zoloft fell out, and landed in the sink.

I felt as if my prayers had been answered. So I picked up the bottle and read the warning label, "*do not over exceed six pills a day. Taking too many antidepressants at once may be life-threatening.*"

I grabbed the bottle and went into the kitchen and got a big glass of water. I then went into my bedroom, looked in the full size mirror that hung on the back of my door, and said, "Lord please forgive me!"

I then took the whole bottle of pills and laid in my bed and patiently waited for my demise.

My eyes got heavy and my body became numb.

All the pain, heartache and disappointments were gone.

Two tears fell from my eyes, as my mind gave one final sigh.

Then I felt nothing. Nothing at all.

My broken soul was finally free.

Unexpectedly, I started smelling various things. My nose was playing tricks on me.

I smelt grandma's peach cobbler, the lasagna mom was eating when I approached her, Tish's body spray, Mel's after shave, Stanley's gym clothes, Kenya's lip gloss, Aunt Jasmine's hair grease, my uncles' barbecue, that

M.A.N.'s cologne, his funky breath, his cigarettes, and then the inside of a hospital.

Suddenly my eyes popped open and I began to vomit.

I tried to sit-up but I couldn't move, because my hands and feet were tied to the bed.

When I realize I was tied down I went ballistic.

I was pulling, kicking, and screaming.

"Untie me!" I shouted.

"Calm down Destiny. We are protecting you," the doctor said.

"You don't understand! You don't understand!" I cried.

Being tied down reminded me of being in that basement.

"I have to get out of here!" I yelled as I continued to aggressively escape.

The doctor gave me a shot to help me relax.

The activated charcoal the doctor gave me to remove the Zoloft out of my system, made me hurl.

All the vomiting I was doing, made me dehydrated.

So when the doctor left, a nurse came into the room, and inserted an intravenous (IV) to rehydrate me.

I was so upset because, I didn't want to be saved. I just kept asking myself, why didn't they let me die? Why didn't God take me, so I wouldn't have to endure anymore pain?

I guess that M.A.N. was right, no one wanted me, not even God. ☹

About an hour later the nurses changed shifts.

When the new nurse on duty checked my blood pressure, heart rate, and lungs, she saw the bruises on my body.

The look on her face was priceless. She quickly documented my bruises and informed the doctor.

Instead of calling the police, the doctor called both mom and that M.A.N. into an office to discuss my bruises. But when the doctor saw that M.A.N. he instantly recognized Reverend Christopher Ogden.

Apparently that M.A.N. preached at his church a few months back, because he was complimenting him on a sermon.

They talked about everything, except my bruises.

That M.A.N. put on his phony Mr. Preacher facade and impressed the doctor even more. After their conversation, the doctor went into my file and disposed of the nurse's report.

Sadly, my bruises were never reported.

What I couldn't understand was how did the doctor and nurses before her not see my physical injuries? And why did the doctor rip up the report?

One of the hardest things for me to do was face my reality, because my reality was, I was in a situation that I would never get help for, because that M.A.N. was well-respected in our community.

So it was my word against his, and my word didn't mean a thing.

The doctor never contacted DCFS; and instead of helping me, they put an ankle bracelet around my ankle to keep track of my every move.

Pretty fucked up right?

But according to the doctor, I had to wear it so they could monitor any future suicide attempts.

I didn't understand how that dumb ankle monitor was going to stop me from killing myself; but again it was a lot about my life I didn't understand.

What the doctors should have done was sent me to a facility that specialized in suicide victims. That way I wouldn't have to be at home with that M.A.N. But unfortunately, they released me into the custody of the person I was trying to escape.

FIGHTING TEMPTATION

Sadly, telling mom and my suicide attempt was unsuccessful and pointless, because it didn't change anything.

That M.A.N. was still physically, verbally, emotionally, and sexually abusing me, even with that dumb ass ankle monitor on.

If that ankle monitor could track a suicide attempt, then why couldn't it track me being abused?

A few weeks after I left the hospital that M.A.N. became a traveling minister.

He often guest spoke at churches in the past, but that was only if the Pastors went out of town or had a special event.

But that was no longer the case.

A huge church, that sponsored several small churches contracted him. So every Sunday that M.A.N. was paid to travel and preach. And Kenya and I were forced to go to church, and watch the phoniness unfold.

I hated watching him stand at a church podium preaching, crying, sweating, shouting, and quoting scriptures. He laid hands on individuals' foreheads and prayed for them. I witnessed saints jumping around the church, fainting, and acting crazy as he spoke in tongues and recited bible verses.

I was disgusted.

That M.A.N. deserved an academy award for his performance.

Hell, he was so good, he damn near fooled me.

When I got home from the hospital, I found out that grandma had a stroke. Stanley criticized me terribly. He called me a dummy for trying to commit suicide. And told me to stop doing selfish shit to seek unnecessary attention, because the family was dealing with enough.

In the midst of all the bullshit he was saying, he informed me that grandma was currently in a Rehabilitation Center trying to recover from her illness. And that my uncles and aunt were doing everything within their power to help her.

Hearing that grandma went through such a tragic situation, broke my heart. I loved my grandma, and she was the only somebody that had my back. I really wish I would've been strong enough to tell her about the abuse, because I'm sure she would have found a way to stop it.

I don't think people realize how hard it is for a child to tell someone that they are being or has been abused. It's very frightening. I mean it's an unbearable fear. You question so many things. Will the person you tell believe you, will they help you, or will they blame you.

Then you have your own guilt that you deal with. Trying to figure out if you did something wrong. All those thoughts have you second guessing yourself and your decision to inform someone. So instead of being or feeling like a victim again, you just suffer in silence.

It is so easy for a person to say what they would or wouldn't do, that has never had to deal with a situation that someone else is forced to deal with.

Grandma said, "never mock a pain you've never endured or judge a situation you've never been in because you will never understand what they're going through. And for all you know, your words could be the last thing they hear before they decide they had enough."

In my case telling someone that M.A.N. was abusing me was even harder. Because he was a reverend, and so many people respected him. And because of that, I was convinced that I wasn't going to receive the help I needed.

It's hard dealing with abuse at any age, but it's even more difficult dealing with it as a helpless child.

Ms. Perkins watched that M.A.N. smack me so hard that it echoed through the hallways, and she did nothing. Tish knew that M.A.N. was an abuser, because he abused her, yet she left Kenya and I there with him, knowing what he was capable of. Kenya knew what he was doing to me and with no remorse at all, she betrayed me. And when I finally got the courage to tell mom, it didn't change anything.

Hell, she consoled that M.A.N., and continued living a fabricated life.

So with no one to help or save me, I was forced to live miserably.

One Thursday when we got home from school Kenya decided to take a nap.

That M.A.N. came in shortly after Kenya went to sleep. When I noticed him I immediately began cleaning. As I swept he sat at the dining room table with his bible, a pen, a highlighter, and a notebook.

The phone rang and he went upstairs to answer it. While he was gone I glanced at the notebook to see what he was writing. That's when I noticed mom's handwriting. I was curious to see what she had written, so I took a closer look.

When I saw that notebook I was a little confused. True enough I didn't know how the church thing worked, but I assumed that the pastor was supposed to find his own message for the week.

I thought reverends had a spiritual relationship with God and He puts a message in their heart to deliver. I didn't "think" that mom was supposed to tell him what to preach about. Not only that…mom only wrote down one verse. So that M.A.N. was going to do what he does best, be a master manipulator by preaching a whole sermon on one sentence, and translate it into what he wanted it to be. And the congregation was going to receive it, and in return scream *Amen, Hallelujah, Thank You Jesus, Glory to God, etc.* And the whole time that M.A.N. will be feeding them a bunch of cow maneuver.

That's why it's important to have your own relationship with God. Cause if you have your own relationship, people can't fool you. They can't pull a wool over your eyes, because you'll be able to recognize the real from the fake.

It's so sad to me how mom and that M.A.N. were comfortable using religion and the Word of God for their own evil gain. And although they appeared to be winning in that moment, one day their winning streak will come to an end.

There is an old saying that says, *"Karma is like a Rubber Band. You only stretch it so far before it come back and smack you in the face."*

As I looked at the notebook I noticed some chicken scratch under mom's handwriting. It looked like a five-year-old child wrote it. It read, "holp is the only ting sronger thin fear."

It took me a minute to understand what it was supposed to say. Once I figured it out I yelled, "Oh…hope is the only thing stronger than fear." I then snickered and mumbled, "his ass doesn't need to call nobody dumb. Who the hell spells hope, h..o..l..p?"

I was so busy giggling that I didn't hear him come down the stairs, so when I looked over my shoulder, he was standing there. I flinched at the sight of him.

Our eyes connected, and he began smiling deceitfully.

That's the same demonic grin he has right before he starts his pedophilia ways.

I quickly turned away, but I felt him watching me. My body was trembling because I was so scared. I knew in a matter of minutes he was going to abuse me, so I rushed to the kitchen to finish cleaning, but I couldn't stop shaking.

He walked behind me, silently grabbed me, and put his hands down my pants. I wanted to run, but my mind and body were working against one another.

I was petrified and my poor body would not stop trembling. That M.A.N.'s devious grin never left his face. The sadness and fear my eyes displayed could not be hidden.

When he unbuttoned my pants, the first tear fell from my eye. He pulled my pants down, the second tear followed. He bent me over, and both the third and fourth tears fell together. Aware of what was about to happen next, I protected myself the best way I knew how. I closed my eyes and allowed my mind to escape my body and wander randomly.

Even through closed eyes, my tears wouldn't stop falling.

I began thinking about my daddy because I knew he would eventually come back for me and rescue me; he had to. He Just Had To! *He was my only hope.*

He picked me up from school, I ran to him with my arms open wide. He swung me around as the wind softly hit my face. When I got in the car, I told him all about my day. He took me to the ice cream parlor. We both got pistachio ice cream. That was my favorite and coincidently it was his as well. I let him read some of my poems and short stories. He expressed how honored he

86

was to call me his daughter. He then told me

how beautiful, smart, and talented I was. And

he apologized for not being a daddy to me

sooner, but he promised to never leave me again,

and gave me a big hug.

My vision faded away because that M.A.N. was done having sex with me.

At least that's what I thought.

I quickly pulled my pants up. I knew something wasn't right because his semen wasn't running down my leg. When I looked at him, I was dumbfounded and speechless. He always had sex with me from the back so I never saw his private parts. So to see that M.A.N. pants still down, and his little penis sticking out his boxer shorts, made me sick to my stomach. His back was against the wall and he was slightly kneeling. The look in his eyes was what confused and frightened me the most. One eye was full of goodness; and the other with wickedness. He was standing before me trying to fight the temptation of molestation.

Have you ever seen a crack addict trying to physically fight their addiction, yet the addiction wins? That's the best way to describe that M.A.N.'s behavior.

I didn't know what to do. *Should I run or stay? If I ran would he catch me and beat me? If I stayed, what would happen to me?*

My mind was clouded. My heart was pounding so fast and hard that I thought it was going to explode inside my chest. Even my tears were confused. They didn't know whether they should fall from my eyes or stay hidden in their tear ducts.

I stood there fearfully unable to move. Suddenly he grabbed me, snatched my pants down, quickly bent me over, stuck his penis in me, and pounded hard and rapidly.

He was carelessly ripping my vaginal tissue. I was in tremendous pain.

I knew it was over when I felt his sperm run down my legs.

When he was done, he pulled up his pants, and yelled, "Why did you let me do that?"

I was too disturbed to look in his direction, too scared to comment, and too angry to understand; so I silently walked away.

I went to the bathroom and looked in the mirror.

Although the fear and pain were visible in my eyes, I did not recognize the face that stared back at me.

I felt dumb, violated, guilty, and frightened.

My heart was aching and my stomach was queasy.

The sight of me, sickened me. I was stupid as hell for allowing that M.A.N. to do that to me. I had a chance to run but my dumb feet would not move.

Why didn't my fucking feet move?

The thought of what just took place was too much for my stomach to handle and I began vomiting.

When I was done I sat on the floor crying.

My vagina was sore and my heart was numb.

I was stuck with so many unanswered questions. So many mental and emotional thoughts occupied my mind.

I took a shower, but I could not get clean.

Once again, the more I washed the dirtier I felt. I scrubbed and scrubbed until my old scabs became new wounds.

But no matter how much soap and water I used, or how hard I washed and scrubbed, my emotions could not be cleansed.

I finally got out of the shower, went to my bedroom, and laid in my bed. I was crying internally and externally. I was in the state of shock. Confusion and disappointment fell from my eyes. I felt guilty, abandoned, betrayed, broken, hopeless, dirty, and hideous.

All I wanted was to be loved and acknowledged by my daddy.

Where was he? Where was my real daddy while that imposter was abusing me?

THE LETTER

I woke up the next day too weak to move.

Tears fell from my eyes as I struggled to get out of bed.

I was in so much pain that I literally had to crawl to the bathroom.

Unfortunately, I didn't make it. And I urinated on myself.

The sad thing was, I could not control my bladder.

I was a strong person, but that day I was broken beyond repair.

So instead of going to clean myself, I crawled to the corner of the wall, put my knees against my chest, buried my head, and cried uncontrollably.

My heart was yearning for my biological daddy, my soul was yearning for Jesus, and my mind was yearning for clarity.

Weeks passed, and I still hadn't seen grandma. I got her phone number from Mel, but every time I called her house, no one answered. I left numerous messages but no one returned my calls. I asked mom could she take me to visit grandma, but she made excuses as to why she couldn't.

I was so crushed.

On top of hurting from not seeing or hearing from grandma, I still had to deal with daily abuse.

I always feared that M.A.N., but due to that psychotic episode he had with himself, I was beyond scared. Because anyone that battles with themselves to that extent, is a different type of dangerous.

What upset me more than his abusive ways, was that he blamed me for his pedophilia behavior. Instead of taking responsibility for his actions, he faults me.

How dare him?

He needs to admit his wrong doings, repent, and ask our Heavenly Father for forgiveness and deliverance.

I could not get that horrible day out of my head. I continuously asked myself, "why didn't you run?" And at one point I agreed with that M.A.N. Had I ran, he wouldn't have had the opportunity to rape me.

That day bothered me so much that I came up with a logical explanation to help me understand and cope with his psychotic behavior.

He was pounding hard and rapidly because he wanted to feed his flesh before his spirit intervened and stopped his pedophiliac conduct. But he allowed his demons to get the best of him, and blamed me because he wasn't man enough to take responsibility for his actions. And in his demonic mind, blaming someone else for his wrongdoings, justified his guilt.

I thought my logical explanation would help soothe my pain, but it didn't. I was hoping and wishing that if I made sense of the situation it would ease my broken heart just a little, but it didn't. I thought telling mom what happened would stop the abuse, but it didn't. I thought if I prayed hard enough it would all go away, but it didn't. I thought that M.A.N. was going to go to jail, but he didn't.

Once again nothing was accomplished, and my faith was fading quickly because I wanted God to hear what I was begging Him for.

Maya Angelou and Langston Hughes were my favorite authors. I read every book and poem they had ever written. I memorized several of their poems. My favorite poems were "I, Too," and "I Know Why the Caged Bird Sings." I loved those poems so much that I taped them to my bedroom wall.

Although I was confused as to why that caged bird sung, I still loved that poem. Maybe because I felt like a caged bird.

"I, Too," poem reminded me that I am someone amazing and my family may not see it now, but one day they'll eventually see just how wonderful I am.

One day Ms. Perkins assigned the class a boring assignment. We had to write a letter to our future self. She wanted our letters to summarize who we were currently, our fears, goals, skills, hobbies, and then give our future self advice.

It was difficult for me to do that assignment because I honestly didn't believe I would have a future. Either I was going to kill myself, or that M.A.N. was going to kill me.

However, I did what I was assigned.

Dear Future Me,

My eighth grade teacher Ms. Perkins assigned the class a stupid assignment today. The assignment is dumb to me because I'm not convinced there will be a future for us? Some girls dream of being beauticians, veterinarians, dancers, choreographers, teachers, mothers, and wives. But I don't have dreams, only nightmares.

I think back to when I used to sit in my bedroom with my favorite doll and cry because my siblings went with their daddies, and I was left at home by myself. Mom wanted to go out so she would drop me off with whomever was willing to take me. I felt like an unwanted burden. And I envied my siblings because they had fathers.

I remember going to grandma's house and she would pray. At the time I just thought she was talking to her dad, because she would always begin her prayers with Heavenly Father. I didn't know who God was back then, but I noticed how the things grandma asked for were granted. No matter what it was. If a friend was sick, she asked and they were healed. If she didn't have money to pay a bill, she asked and it was paid. I used to say to myself, "man her dad is excellent. I wish I had a father like that. Let me start asking my daddy for things." So I would ask for things the same way grandma did, and start each sentence with, "Heavenly Father." Unbeknownst to me I was praying.

One day grandma explained to me what prayer was, but I didn't understand who God was, maybe because I was still under the impression that she was talking to her earthly father.

I would often say, "Heavenly Father, may you please be the daddy I want and need, and if I can't have You, may you please send me a replacement?" Well one day He answered my prayers and put that M.A.N. in my life. I regret praying that prayer every single day.

Every time I see that M.A.N.'s face I am constantly reminded that I prayed for him. I wish I would have stayed fatherless. Or that God would have sent me a better father and not that M.A.N. Every single day I wish I could unpray that prayer, and every single day I pray the opposite of what I prayed before, because I want that M.A.N. out of MY LIFE!

Sadly, my prayers have gone unanswered and each day brings me more pain than the last. I wake up wondering is today the day that I will be missed or mourned? Or will today be the day I'm rescued?

I hate my life. I don't think I am good enough, pretty enough, or smart enough. People around me has me questioning my every move, in fear of being bullied, criticized, or beaten. I cry myself to sleep every night. And lately I'm not crying about what I'm going through, I'm crying because I hate that I am so weak and scary. I honestly feel like I'm in prison, a prison that was created by my fears. Had I been more courageous, you wouldn't have to endure the aftermath of my cowardliness.

I pretend to be strong, when I'm really weak. However, I cannot let others know just how weak I am or how much pain I'm in, because they'll use that against me. And that will put an even bigger target on my back. So, I just walk around with my head down not giving anyone direct eye contact, because I'm worried that my silent tears will be visible.

I'm forced to live a lie, I'm forced to smile, and I'm forced to hide my internal pain. I wish someone would look close enough to see just how broken I really am inside. I wish someone would recognize my physical and emotional wounds, then maybe they can help me before it's too late. But no one seems to notice the way my body tense up when that M.A.N. comes around, or how I don't give direct eye contact when someone talks to me, or how I don't change for gym class, even after being punished by the gym teacher. Instead everyone goes on with their lives, my wounds go unnoticed, and I'm left emotionally drowning in soundless tears.

One day at lunch, a classmate randomly criticized me from head to toe. Then he said, "Destiny is broke as hell." (Broke is a slang term for poor). Of course he got some laughs at the expense of my pain; but the laughs didn't bother me, the truth is what hurt me.

I am broke!!! And I'm not talking poor neither. I am internally broken, and my innocent little heart is unable to heal because a piece of me breaks each day. I feel like the weight of the world is on my shoulders and I don't know what to do to get out from under it.

I live with so much regret because never in a million years would I imagined that an innocent prayer would cause us so much pain and change our life forever. Due to my prayer, we are forever changed and trusting anyone else is not an option. Now I carry the burden of shame and blame, and I apologize for what I've put you through. Had I been strong enough, you wouldn't have to deal with the aftermath of my fearfulness.

I hope and pray that you are stronger than I am. I hope you can stop the fire from burning in the hell that I am currently living in. I pray you have the courage to confront mom with your true feelings and standup to that M.A.N. and all the bullies of the world, because I'm sure as hell is too weak to do so. I hope that someday the scars on your heart heals faster than the ones on my body. I pray that your faith in God and your faith in yourself doesn't dry up like a raisin in the sun. I hope that when you look in the mirror you will see a beautiful woman that is happy despite of. I pray that you prove everyone that doubted you wrong. I hope that you learn how to love yourself. I pray that someday you will know who you are, what your purpose in life is, what you are worth, and what you deserve.

I hope that you never turn into the bitter

hatred people around you. I pray that you

learn to protect yourself since no one else was

willing to protect you. And I hope you find

your light, and let it shine despite the

darkness that I am now facing.

~Ms. Invisible

When I turned in my assignment, I prayed that Ms. Perkins would look beyond the ink and see that I was desperately crying for help.

When Kenya and I got home from school that M.A.N. was sitting in the living room with that thick piece of wood on the side of him. I hadn't seen that stick since he accidently broke it while beating me.

I could not believe that fool fixed that stick by wrapping electric tape around it.

He immediately invented an excuse to chastise me. I knew he was lying, but I went to the dungeon anyway because he was so unpredictable. Even more so now because I told mom about the abuse.

That M.A.N. took me to the basement, beat me, and raped me. I don't know what mom expected to achieve by making me and Kenya come home together.

She couldn't possibly think that my "little" sister would protect me from him. So I was confused as to what she was trying to accomplish?

All she did was made him find creative ways to fulfill his addiction.

I thought of numerous ways to commit suicide, because I was so tired of living that miserable life.

My life was full of unanswered questions.

I once read that, *"an unanswered question is better than an unquestioned answered."* I still don't know what that means. I wish I did, cause maybe it could help me understand my life.

I was so lost. My heart was hollow and my soul was dark. Why was God always answering grandma's prayers, but not mine? The one prayer that He should have ignored, He granted.

Why won't mom leave that M.A.N. alone? What was it about him that made her stay?

I felt so betrayed. I wanted to trust mom, but I couldn't. I tried to obey God's Word, but I couldn't help but feel He was responsible. Why would He make things so hard for me? Ironically my abuser was a man of God.

How could I trust a God that has ordained a pedophile to deliver His Word to the world?

I was so confused. Everything I thought was right, turned out to be wrong.

People seek God when they are emotionally distress, they go to church when they need their joy refilled, and they turn to the bible when they need guidance. But to watch that M.A.N. represent all three, made me question the God I was praying to.

Unfortunately, with no one to turn to, and nowhere else to go, my faith was deteriorating, and sadly there was nothing I could do about it. The one person I should be able to go to for help, had shown me several times why I could not go to her.

However, she was my only hope. If only I could get her to open her eyes and see beyond that M.A.N.'s disguise, then maybe, just maybe, I'll have a chance.

But how could I accomplish such a thing? When I told her about her husband abusing me, nothing changed.

Hopefully Ms. Perkins feel my pain through my letter and help me.

As I began thinking about Ms. Perkins and her current assignment, it triggered a thought. If I could write a letter to my future self exposing my feelings. Then I could write a letter to mom doing the same.

I got my journal from under my mattress and began writing a letter to mom.

Dear mom,

I barely get any sleep at night because I am terrified of your husband. He still finds ways to beat me, and have sex with me. I'm not strong enough to stop him, and I do not feel safe around him. Had I known informing you wouldn't have changed my situation I would have kept my mouth shut, because I'm now living in fear. I believe he is going to kill me; he's just waiting for the perfect opportunity.

Mom I don't understand, how someone so beautiful, professional, and well educated as yourself, can turn your back on the evil doings of your husband. How could you allow your

husband to be so mischievous? And how do
you sleep with him at night knowing that he
finds pleasure in having sex with children?
And not just any children, but the child you
birth!

You do realize you're just as guilty as he
is, if not guiltier, because you have the power
to stop him. Yet you ignore what you know in
your heart is true. Whatever happens to me,
my blood is on your hands, because you are
aware of the situation, and you did nothing to
stop it.

Your Abused Child,

Destiny

I ripped the letter out of my journal, put it in a small
envelope, and in the morning when I took them their
coffee, I stuck it in mom's purse.

That night when mom got home from work, she didn't mention the letter. I began to wonder; did she receive it?

Maybe that M.A.N. went into her purse and removed the letter before she saw it.

I wrote mom a letter every day, put it in a small envelope, and stuck it in her purse.

For two weeks I wrote her, and sadly she never addressed nor acknowledged any of my letters. I was worried, because I didn't know if mom had received my letters or if she was deliberately avoiding them.

I finally gave up because I felt writing her was irrelevant. Then I thought about the movie, "The Color Purple." *Ms. Celie sister wrote her once a week for years, and despite never receiving a reply, she never gave up. She just stopped writing once a week and wrote on holidays, in hopes that Mister would have the holiday spirit and give Ms. Celie her letters.*

Although Ms. Celie didn't receive the letters when they were written, she did eventually get them.

Reminiscing on that movie motivated me to write another letter.

Dear mom,

I wrote you numerous letters, and I have yet to receive a response. Did you receive them? If so, please acknowledge it.

That night when mom got home from work she knocked on my bedroom door. When I opened it, she said, "I enrolled you and Kenya in an after-school program at the Community Center," then she turned and walked away.

I wasn't pleased with her delivery; however, I was happy she made a minor modification in my life. So we wouldn't have to be at home with that M.A.N.

Our first day at the Community Center was fun. It was a great and peaceful environment. I was able to finish my homework, help others with their work, play games, do arts and crafts, socialize with other children my age, and watch old reruns of the television series Law and Order.

The Community Center closed at six o'clock. When they were closing Kenya and I left to walk home. But when we got outside that M.A.N. was waiting on us. His presence startled me. I grabbed Kenya's hand in hopes of protecting her, but she snatched away and got in the van. So I followed.

My heart was pounding loud and hard. I looked at both Kenya and that M.A.N. wondering if they could hear the noise coming from my chest. My stomach was going up and down as if I was on a roller coaster. My thoughts were scattered and blurry. I was petrified because I wasn't sure if he had read the letters I wrote to mom.

That M.A.N. turned the radio up as loud as it could go, and then turned left when he was supposed to turn right. I instantly began panicking.

"Where are you taking us? Why aren't we going home?" I screamed.

I tried to open the door, but the child proof locks were on.

"Open this door!!!" I cried, while pulling on the van's door handle and beating on the window.

Kenya looked at me as if I was insane. Tears rolled down my face as my heart continued to pound.

That M.A.N. was about to kill us and I needed to escape. So I took my seatbelt off and started kicking the window, praying that it would break, so I could jump out.

"Destiny Stop!" Kenya screamed.

"We got to get out of here! Help me dammit!" I yelled.

Kenya would not help me, instead she sat there with her seatbelt on, trying to figure out what was wrong with me.

That M.A.N. Was About To Kill Us!!!

She didn't understand the severity of the situation, but I did.

My legs were aching and the pain had become too unbearable, so I stopped kicking.

I slowly sat down and quietly looked at that M.A.N.

He was emotionless and quiet. He didn't say anything, not even when I tried to kick the window out. That made me even more frightened.

Once I realized there was nothing I could do, I put my feet in the seat, buried my head between my knees, and fearfully wept.

As I sat there crying I heard the van door open. I jumped up ready to fight for my life.

I was going to scratch and bite the hell out of that M.A.N., that way the police would have his DNA, when the medical examiner examines my body.

However, when I jumped up to fight, I saw mom get in the van. Seeing her was a relief. My heart, mind, and body slowly calmed down. I wiped my face and buckled my seat belt.

When we got home I immediately wrote mom a letter,

Dear mom,

Kenya and I can walk home from the Community Center. No need for your husband to pick us up. Thanks in advance.

The next day before we left the Community Center I peeked out the door and saw the van. I grabbed Kenya by the hand and told her we're walking. We exited through the back door and took a different route home.

When that M.A.N. and mom got home they approached me right away. As usual that M.A.N. did all the talking.

"Where were you today?"

"School," I replied.

"Where did you go after school?"

"The Community Center."

"No, you didn't."

"Okay," I replied while shrugging my shoulders.

"So, where the hell were you?" That M.A.N. yelled.

"The Community Center," I repeated.

That M.A.N. then looked at mom and said, "See I told you not to let them go to that after school program. She uses that as an excuse to mess with those little nappy headed boys."

I shook my head and calmly said, "that's not what I'm doing?"

"Yeah that's exactly what you are doing!" He yelled.

I looked at mom and said, "you can call the director tomorrow to confirm our whereabouts."

That M.A.N. stood there mean-mugging me. I knew he was trying to intimidate me, but it didn't work. I just looked at mom and asked, "are we done here?"

"Hell Naw we aren't done!" He yelled.

"Wow…is that how a man of God supposed to talk?" I asked.

"Destiny stop being disrespectful, and tell me why you were not outside when I got there?" He shouted.

I calmly replied, "I guess you weren't properly informed, but Kenya and I will be walking home. Sorry you weren't notified in advance."

Both that M.A.N. and I looked at mom, she stood there mutely dazed. She then broke her silence by replying, "the girls will walk home from now on."

I looked at that M.A.N., rolled my eyes, and

skipped to my bedroom, because finally mom didn't

disappoint me.

A week later Ms. Perkins graded our future letters.

She gave me a **B+**. With a note that read:

"Your letter was quite interesting. Unfortunately, you

did not list your hobbies nor give advice to your future self.

For those reasons alone, your grade has decreased."

I was sad, because I really hoped she would look

beyond the assignment, feel my pain, and hear my cries for

help.

THE KNIFE IN MY BACK

Mom surprised me when she complied with my request. I finally felt that she was using the good sense God blessed her with. I had faith that things were going to get better. However, I continued writing her letters and putting them in her purse.

The letters were just expressing how I felt daily. Mom had become my second journal. I told her about the physical and verbal bullying I endured at school. And that her husband was the reason I was bullied when he made me lie on two of my classmates.

I described the emotional suffering I dealt with daily, due to that M.A.N. violating me. I expressed how not knowing my real daddy, left a hole in my heart. I explained how that M.A.N. still found ways to whip and molest me, and that prison was the only thing that would stop his pedophilia ways.

I wrote mom for eighteen days, and she hadn't acknowledged any of my letters. However, the senseless beatings and sexual abuse stopped. I was grateful for that.

Nevertheless, I continued writing her. And although she never verbalized anything to me, I knew my letters triggered something inside of her that made her feel and think outside of her selfishness.

I thought things were getting better, but then the unexpected happened.

One Friday when mom got home from work, she was exhausted. Her eyes were swollen and puffy, and it looked as if she hadn't slept in days. *Mom's guilt was killing her.*

I was in the kitchen washing dishes when she approached me.

"When you are done cleaning meet me in my bedroom," she said.

Before I could respond, she disappeared. Unaware of mom's intentions I went to her bedroom. Luckily that M.A.N. was not around.

"Have a seat," she said.

I hesitated for a moment, because I honestly didn't trust mom and I hated their bedroom, due to the horrific memories.

The same room she shared with her husband, was the same room he robbed me, and the same room she betrayed me.

"What's wrong?" Mom asked.

"What do you mean?" I questioned

"Destiny Baby have a seat." *Baby! Did she just call me baby?*

I refused to sit on her bed, so I grabbed their clothes hamper, turned it upside down, and sat on it.

"Do you really want your dad to go to jail?" She asked.

"My dad? You mean your husband?"

"Do you want him to go to jail?" She repeated with an attitude.

"Yes," I answered.

"Why?" Mom asked.

She could not possibly be this dumb.

"What do you mean why? Because your husband is a pedophile."

"He made a mistake."

"A mistake? Are you serious? So, was Tish a mistake to?"

"He didn't have sex with Tish."

"Wow…so you're acknowledging that you are aware that your husband had sex with me, yet you're trying to convince me that him molesting, raping, and beating me repeatedly was a mistake. And what he did to Tish is excusable because he didn't stick his raggedy penis in her? So let me ask you this, if what he did to me was a mistake, what do you call what he did to Tish? And what will you call it when he does it to Kenya?"

Mom paused momentarily, then she replied, "Destiny things look bad now, but we'll get through this. Just think about it and make sure this is what you want."

I was confused and offended. I felt like I was trapped in the movie "Invasion of the Body Snatchers," because mom could not be that damn stupid. That M.A.N. had to put some type of voodoo on her, because the mumbo jumbo that was exiting her mouth wasn't making sense.

Mom words left me speechless and hurt. I felt abandoned. I felt hopeless. And I felt broken. Who was I supposed to turn to when the only person in the world that could stop me from hurting, was the one hurting me?

I closed my eyes and covered my face with my hands.

"Destiny!" Mom called.

"WHAT!" I shouted.

"Your dad is a good man."

"Mom just stop! Please stop!" I begged.

"Destiny look at what he does for the community, and how he…"

I interrupted her immediately, "I'm not about to let you put perfume on cow manure and tell me it's not dookie, cause no matter how you dress it up, it's still BULLSHIT! I don't care what he does for the community, all I care about is what he has done to me. Then to add insult to injury you're trying to convince me that the abuse I endured was a mistake, and I need to suck it up because he's a pillar of the community! Mom how? How am I supposed to get over something so devastating? The sad thing is, you know the truth but you don't want to accept it because you don't want your reputation destroyed. But how do you sleep at night knowing that you are an accomplice to sexual and physical abuse of a child? It saddens me to my core how you are willing to sell your soul to the devil in the name of love."

"This has nothing to do with love!" She yelled.

I took a deep breath and said, "so help me understand, if it's not about love, then what is it about?

"Our family!"

I briefly stared at her and said, "Wow!!! Our family huh? You do realize that we no longer have a family! Our family broke up the day you said I do to that M.A.N. Your children are all scattered and divided. You and Aunt Jasmine relationship has vanished like a thief in the night. Grandma is sick and you have yet to take us to see her. We don't see our uncles anymore, and Tish and Mel despise you. So help me understand what family you're referring to?"

Mom did not answer.

"You must be talking about your church family," I said.

Again she was speechless.

So I continued, "that M.A.N...your husband...the person you forced your children to call dad...took pieces of my life that I can never get back. And you stand before me, telling me the only reason he's not being penalized for his actions is because you want to keep your family together. PEARL YOU NO LONGER HAVE A FAMILY!!!"

The more I talked the madder I became. I respected mom, even when she did not respect me. But I had been silent for too long, so that day I boldly verbalized my pain.

I looked her right in those puffy eyes and waited for a response. She put her head down, because she was too ashamed to give me direct eye contact. It was evident that she wasn't going to say anything. So I got up from the hamper and continued, "You know damn well this is not about family, it's about keeping up that fake façade you and your husband has going on. You love being referred to as "The First Lady." And you love being able to say you are the famous Reverend Ogden's wife, because it makes you feel special and important. It's really sad how you are more worried about the naysayers than you are the safety and wellbeing of your children. You would do anything to keep your truth a secret. From killing yourself at work, to justifying that M.A.N.'s pedophilia ways."

"So, you don't think this hurt me?" Mom cried.

"You're not too hurt because you trying to convince me why your husband doesn't deserve to go to jail. What is pissing me off is, you know the truth, yet you aren't doing anything about it. Maybe you don't realize how bad the abuse was. Or maybe you just don't want to realize it. Maybe you can't accept that you married a pervert, so you make excuses and justifications to ease your guilt. I just wish you knew how much damage your husband has caused me mentally, emotionally, and physically. Then maybe, just maybe, you would send him to jail."

Mom sat there expressionless. I don't know what I expected her response to be, I just wanted one. I didn't care if it was negative or positive. I needed confirmation that my words had not falling on deaf ears. Sadly, she said nothing. Not one word. I waited for her to look at me, hug me, yell, cry, smile; any reaction would have helped me understand how she was feeling at that moment. I took one last look at her, and then I walked out her bedroom.

As I exit she shouted, "I told your dad you talked to the school counselor about the situation?"

I turned around and screamed, "HE IS NOT MY DAMN DADDY!!!"

She ignored me and continued, "Your dad is in the family room and he wants to talk with you. I informed him that you want him to go to prison."

Tears dripped from my eyes, as pain poured from my heart.

"Would you like me to pull it out now or later?" I cried.

"Pull out what?"

"The knife you shoved in my back and jabbed in my heart!"

"What are you talking about?"

"I begged you to help me. I begged you to protect me. I begged you to love me. I begged you to find my daddy. I begged you for my daddy's name. I begged you to put that M.A.N. out. I begged you to send him to jail. I begged you to take me to see my grandma. Yet no matter how much I begged, pleaded, and cried, you ignored and betrayed me. And I don't understand why. I pray one day you will un-break my heart, but obviously today is not that day."

"Destiny please talk to him," she begged.

I was furious. My palms were sweating, body temperature decreased, my breathing increased, my head and heart were racing, as I clenched my jaw. I wanted to punch the fuck out of her. *How dare she beg me to talk to that bitch?*

I stared into her eyes making my pain and anger visible. "Not only did you lie on me to that M.A.N., but you can't even say it...You have yet to acknowledge what your husband has repeatedly done to me. Stop referring to it as *"SITUATION"* And Acknowledge What He Did!!! Acknowledge That He Raped Me, Molested Me, Violated Me, Attacked Me, Abused Me, Beat Me, Embarrassed Me, Shamed Me, Robbed Me, Smacked Me, Kicked Me, Punched Me, Bullied Me, Criticized Me, Blamed Me, Tortured Me...And you want me to talk to him!!! For What? About What? What could he possibly say to me that will correct his wrongs? What could he possibly tell me that will give me back my virginity? His punk ass thinks he's going to jail and now he has a conscious. Now he's apologetic? Where was his conscious at when he was forcing his dick in my premature vagina? Where was his conscious when he was beating me like a slave on a plantation? FUCK HIS CONSCIOUS, FUCK HIS PEDOPHILE LIFE, AND FUCK YOU TO!!!"

"Stop cursing like you're grown and just go see what he has to say!" Mom yelled.

My heart was still racing, and her words and unsympathetic behavior infuriated me even more. But instead of doing something foolish, I just walked away.

I didn't want to see that M.A.N. so I used the front staircase to avoid the family room. But when I walked down the stairs he was sitting on the living room couch with his head down and his hands together as if he was praying. He lifted his head when he heard my footsteps. Our eyes connected.

"Come here!" He demanded.

I rolled my eyes, smacked my lips, and continued walking to my bedroom. He jumped off the couch, ran behind me, and grabbed my arm.

I pushed him as hard as I could and yelled, "keep your motherfucking hands to yourself!"

Then I calmly walked to my bedroom, slammed the door, and blasted the radio.

That night I heard mom and that M.A.N. arguing. I didn't know what they were arguing about, but I felt it was pertaining to me. So, I turned my radio down, and put my ear to the door. During the argument I heard mom say, "How would you feel if I cheated on you with your son?"

Her words knocked the air out of me and I was suffocating with each breath I took. I felt my heart literally break into pieces. I grabbed my chest and slowly slid down the wall as tears streamed down my face. My silent tears turned into mild sobs, and my mild sobs turned into loud cries.

Every tear I cried, every letter I wrote, and every word I spoke, didn't mean a damn thing to her. Dumb bitch thinks her husband cheated "with me." How is that even possible? If she feels her hypocritical pedophile ass husband cheated on her, with me, then how does she feel about me? Is she blaming me for being abused?

How could she even allow those words to exit her mouth? I was robbed of my fucking innocents and she asking this fool how would he feel? BITCH what about me? What about my feelings? Her husband, Reverend Christopher Ogden ruined my life, by molesting, raping, beating, and abusing me, and she thinks she was cheated!!! NO SELFISH BITCH!!! I WAS THE ONE CHEATED!!!

RADIO STATION

Things got a little better after a while. That M.A.N. continued living in the house with us, but the physical and sexual abuse stopped completely.

Whenever I was home I stayed in my bedroom with the door locked.

I didn't watch much television because I didn't have one in my bedroom. And the only time I left my room was to shower, use the bathroom, eat, or do my chores.

I barely looked in the mirror because I didn't like what I saw. I guess all the criticism I received over the years affected me mentally.

That M.A.N. went from being a traveling reverend, to preaching on a Christian radio station. Mom and that M.A.N. teamed up with mom's friend, Ms. Truman to do a radio ministry. Ms. Truman's job was to tell listeners where to send their donations, but that was short lived because Ms. Truman quit a few weeks later. And we never saw her again.

Mom did all the reading on air, while that M.A.N. explained the verse(s) she read. I honestly didn't listen to them, because I knew the truth behind those sermons.

One evening that M.A.N. and mom made us listen to a taping of their radio ministry. As we sat and listened I started giggling.

Kenya, Stanley, that M.A.N., and mom all looked at me. They were confused as to why I was laughing. The more they stared, the harder I giggled.

I thought about the day Tish slammed the bible shut and cursed that M.A.N. out. For the first time, I understood exactly how she felt, because I wanted to grab that tape out of the cassette player and break it.

Sadly, not even the Word of God was strong enough to shake that M.A.N.'s addiction. Cause shortly after their radio ministry was established, the evilness resurfaced.

Their phoniness aired on the gospel station at 2:00 a.m. Sunday mornings. And between the hours of midnight and 1:00am, that M.A.N. woke me up to make their coffee.

While I was making their coffee, he came behind me and rubbed my breast. I was going to tell mom, but for what? She didn't do anything before, so why would she do anything now? Besides mom had too much to lose, so to avoid being disappointed, I just kept quiet.

Rubbing my breast became a Sunday morning routine. And although I could not believe that M.A.N. was back to his old ways, I could honestly say I was not surprised.

However, I was flabbergasted at how bold he was. He was downstairs molesting me, while his wife was upstairs getting ready to go to the radio station, where he preached the Word of God to strangers.

That M.A.N. could care less about consequences, because he was obviously going to feed his pedophilic addiction by any means necessary.

One Sunday I must've went into disassociation mode when that M.A.N. put his hand in my shirt because I didn't remember him putting his hand down my pajama pants. I assume the sound of the coffee pot beeping made me snap back to reality. While he was fingering my vagina, I grabbed the coffee pot and purposely dropped it. The glass shattered and hot coffee went everywhere. Without saying a word, he took his hand out my pants and smacked me.

"What was that?" Mom said running into the kitchen.

"Her stupid butt broke our coffee pot!" That
M.A.N. yelled.

I stood there holding my face as tears streamed
down my cheeks. Mom looked at me and asked,
"how did you do that?"

But before I could answer that M.A.N. quickly
intervened and said, "we'll buy another one tomorrow.
Let's leave a few minutes early so we can stop somewhere
and grab some coffee."

Mom only response was "okay."

Not once did she question why I was standing in the
kitchen holding my face with tears running down my
cheeks. And why was it okay for him to wake me up out
my sleep to make their damn coffee?

It was at that moment that I realize no one was
going to save me.

So I had to learn how to be my own super hero and
rescue myself.

When mom and that M.A.N. left I could not sleep. So I pulled out my journal and wrote a letter to God.

Dear Heavenly Father,

I am sad, angry, irritated, and frustrated. That M.A.N. is back to his old ways. How could this be Father? Just when I think things change for the better, reality slaps me in the face. I guess I'm the one to blame, because I knew he didn't change, yet and still I wanted to believe he did.

Here I am hoping and praying that I would finally have a normal life. But I knew in my heart that my life would never be normal, especially while I'm still living in the house with my abuser. Seeing his face every day is a mockery. Cause I'm constantly reminded that I don't matter, and he can do

140

whatever he wants to me and there will be no consequences for his actions.

He disgusts me. The sound of his voice, his face, the smell of his cologne, his funky breath, and his fraudulent facade makes me sick to my stomach. Because no matter how much of Your Word he preaches, no matter how many tears he shed, no matter how many spiritual tongues he speaks, and no matter how many times he pretends to catch the holy ghost. He is still the same creepy pedophile.

Father I am upset with You. How can I serve You, when You are the one that place that M.A.N. in my life, and allowed him to do all the things he has done to me? I feel I am being punished for something, and I don't understand what I've done and why my punishment has to be so harsh. I wish I had more answers and a better understanding as to why I am in this situation, but I don't, and my anger and bitterness is growing because I can't figure it out.

Father I am extremely tired. And allowing that M.A.N. to abuse and degrade me is no longer an option.

Father as my last plea for help, please get me out this situation and get that M.A.N. out my life forever.

That M.A.N. preached quite well, but he was nothing more than a wolf in sheep's clothing. A false prophet is what the bible calls them.

Grandma said, "it's not the messenger, it's the message."

But how many people will actually take his message(s) serious if they knew he was a child molesting prick?

I hate to admit it, but that M.A.N. helped a lot of people through troubled situations in their lives. It was just sad that he couldn't help himself.

Listening to that M.A.N. pray for others made me sad, angry, and question God. Every day I became more heartless. My hate for him grew stronger and stronger. I wanted him to die. I wanted him to die a long painful death.

Mom bought a new coffee pot and like clockwork, that M.A.N. woke me up Sunday morning, a little after midnight to make their coffee. I was tired and irritated, but I got out of bed. I washed my hands and prepared their coffee. That M.A.N. stood right next to me watching my every move. So I turned around and asked, "why do you always have to wake me up? Why don't you just make your own coffee?"

"Stop being disrespectful and do as you are told," he replied.

So I made their coffee like I was demanded. But I didn't make it like I normally did. When he left to check on mom, I put a little dishwashing liquid in the coffee filter.

When he came downstairs, he walked behind me, and rubbed my breast. I quickly turned around, smacked his hands, and yelled, "Stop touching me!!!"

Rage filled his eyes, as we stood face to face, having a staring match. I don't know what I was thinking at the time, or if I was thinking at all, because I saw his lips moving, but I didn't hear a word exit his mouth. That M.A.N. raised his hand to hit me and I grabbed his wrist. I looked him dead in the eyes and screamed, "YOU DON'T SCARE ME!"

The thought of losing his power infuriated him. He snatched his wrist from my grip and head-butted me right between the eyes. I was dizzy and my sight became blurry for a few seconds. I fought to maintain my balance, but before I could, he smacked me.

I fell down and was struggling to get up.

That M.A.N. charged at me with full force. So I quickly laid back and started kicking my feet fast and uncontrollably.

He kept trying to smack my legs so that I would stop kicking, but in the midst of him doing that. One of my kicks landed in his chest, which caused him to slightly fall back. Although the kick didn't hurt him, it gave me an opportunity to make my next move. So I quickly jumped up, grabbed his penis, and twisted it as hard as I could. "I OWN MY BODY! NOT YOU OR ANYONE ELSE!!!" I shouted, as he fell to his knees in pain, begging me to let his manhood go. Veins were popping out his neck and forehead.

When I finally released his penis, I jumped up, kicked him in the chin, ran in my bedroom, and locked the door.

PROVOKED

It was very common for me to wake up in the middle of the night, but that night was different. I opened my eyes because I felt something in my room.

My bedroom was dark except for the nightlight that I kept next to my night stand. I saw a shadow move from the door to my bed. I assumed it was a figment of my imagination because I made sure my bedroom door was locked before I went to sleep.

Maybe I was just paranoid.

I rubbed my eyes, and when I put my hands down, that M.A.N.'s face appeared. I screamed, but he quickly put his hand over my mouth. I grabbed his face and pushed my thumbs deep into his eyeballs. He let my mouth go and grabbed my hands. I yelled for help, so he put a pillow over my head to mute the screams. Although my cries couldn't be heard, I continued yelling and fighting. I scratched his arms and hands to get him to release the pillow. He put his knees on my arms to stop me from attacking him. I was helpless and scared. Tears rolled out the side of my eyes as I fought to breathe. I stopped screaming and fighting, and I started praying, until I passed out.

The sound of my alarm clock woke me up. I looked around my bedroom and exhaled. *It was just a dream!* When I got out of bed I was in my underwear and my vagina was sore.

I questioned did I get hot and take my pants off. I knew that wasn't something I would normally do, but I second guessed myself, because I was confused and honestly couldn't remember.

Once I was done taking my shower, I got dressed, and put a pop tart in the toaster. I glanced at the clock and noticed it was getting late. I needed to hurry because I had to meet Myeisha.

I got the pop tart out the toaster, wrapped it in a napkin, and grabbed my backpack. I was headed out the door when I saw that M.A.N, and he was staring at me hatefully. He was wearing a long sleeve shirt so I couldn't see his arms. But when I looked at his hands, I noticed the scratches. Every bone in my body tensed up because I realized that last night was not a dream.

That M.A.N. was physically in my bedroom and tried to suffocate me with my pillow.

I flared my nose, sucked my teeth, threw my pop tart at him, and ran out the front door.

I was pissed. The thought of him breaking into my bedroom in the middle of the night and putting a pillow over my head infuriated me.

He had to rape me. Why else would my vagina be sore?

I was stuck questioning that M.A.N.'s intentions. *What was he trying to accomplish? Was he trying to kill me? Did he think I was dead? Or did he rape me?*

I felt that M.A.N.'s motives were to recommence my fear. He needed me afraid of him, because pedophiles preyed on the weak. Sadly, that M.A.N. didn't just prey on the weak, he also prayed for the weak.

But what he failed to realize was, I wasn't that same little weak girl he once took advantage of. All the things he did to me over the years made me resilient. Pain made me stronger, fear made me braver, and failure made me wiser. So, his actions didn't create a scaredy-cat, it birthed a fearless beast.

When I left I didn't go to Myeisha's house. Instead I took a different route to school. I just needed to be alone.

Once I got to school the kids were lining up to go inside. I walked to the end of the line and stood against the brick building. When other children approached the line, I let them go ahead of me, because I wasn't ready to go inside just yet.

In the midst of me standing there, Myeisha's dad pulled up. Myeisha reached over and gave him a hug and a kiss on the cheek. She then jumped out the car smiling and uttering the words, "I love you to daddy."

Watching them made my blood boil with envy.

When Myeisha saw me, she walked to the end of the line to greet me.

"Hey Destiny, I went to your house and your mom said you left already."

"I did," I replied with an attitude.

"Why didn't you come get me so we could walk to school together?"

"You were fine, your daddy brought you."

"Did I do something wrong?" She asked.

"What do you mean?"

"You're acting like you're upset with me."

"No, you're good," I said as I walked in the school.

Myeisha went to her classroom and I went to mine.

I sat in class all day and didn't do any assignments.

When it was time for lunch, I stood in line, got my tray of food, and sat down.

I didn't eat anything because I was still distraught.

I could not get that M.A.N. out of my head. I was so mad at myself for not remembering all the details.

Did he rape me, and if so why didn't I wake up? My thoughts were interrupted when Myeisha sat in the chair across from me. She was holding a McDonald's bag and cup.

"My daddy didn't have to work today so he surprised me with lunch."

"Congratulations," I replied sarcastically.

"Do you want some?"

"No!"

"Destiny are you okay? You don't seem like yourself today."

"That's cause I'm not."

"What's wrong? Did that M.A.N. do something to you?" She whispered.

I looked around the cafeteria to see if anyone was paying attention to our conversation. I observed kids in the corner playing the game Truth or Dare, I saw the security guard flirting with the lunch lady, and I noticed other children holding random conversations.

Once I realized no one was paying attention to us I whispered to Myeisha, "yes. Last night he…" But before I could tell her what happened, a boy name Quinton sat next to her.

"Hey Myeisha," he said.

"Hello Quinton."

Not once did he speak to me or even acknowledged my presence. I didn't care though because I was still trying to figure out if that M.A.N. raped me.

As he sat and talked to Myeisha I noticed some of the other kids snickering, whispering, and watching. By that time, I knew they dared him to do something foolish, I just assumed he was going to kiss Myeisha and run. So, I rested my elbows on the table, and covered my face with my hands, until he left.

"Can I have a French fry?" Quinton asked Myeisha

"You can have the rest," Myeisha said handing him the box of fries.

"Thank you," he said politely.

He took a fry out of the box, ate it, and then called my name. When I looked up to see what he wanted, that fool threw the rest of the French fries in my face.

Before I had a chance to think, I reacted. I grabbed my plastic lunch tray and hit him in the face with it.

He fell out the chair and food went everywhere. I jumped over the table and kept hitting him while yelling, "I'm tired of people fucking with me!"

Quinton was on the floor covering his face.

Myeisha was begging me to stop, while trying to pull me off of him.

"Get off of me!" I yelled as I hit her with the tray.

All the other kids were crowded around us, laughing and instigating. One teacher tried to grab me, and got injured in the process.

Finally, security came and literally picked me up and carried me out the cafeteria.

I was still yelling, kicking, cursing, and swinging that tray like a maniac.

Security carried me all the way to Ms. Jefferson office. She called mom at work and informed her that I was suspended for five days, due to my erratic behavior.

After she explained the situation to mom, she gave me the telephone.

"Destiny why am I getting calls at work regarding your behavior?" Mom asked.

"Mom she isn't telling you the entire story. That boy threw French fries in my face, for no reason. And I'm getting punished for defending myself. That's not fair."

"Destiny you injured that boy, a teacher, and your friend. What did you expected to happen?"

"Mom I didn't mean to hurt Myeisha or Ms. Kathy, but Quinton provoked me! I told you that I was being bullied and you did nothing about it, so I handled it myself."

"Destiny, calm down."

"No, I am not going to calm down, because he provoked me. The same way your husband keeps provoking me. I am tired of being everyone's pincushion."

"Destiny we will talk about this when I get home."

"No mom, we need to talk now. You need to set up a meeting with Ms. Jefferson and Quinton's parents so that we can get this issue resolved. Cause if I'm getting suspended he needs to get suspended to. He is only getting one day detention for throwing fries in my face! Why is his punishment so lenient, but mines so severe? And don't think I'm staying home with that M.A.N. either, because I'm not! And if you try to make me…"

"I said we will talk about it when I get home!" Mom yelled.

"Whatever!" I said as I aggressively hung up the phone.

I am sick and tired of people using me. Whether it's to fulfill their addiction, gain kudos from the popular kids, or mask their own insecurities. It's funny how society questions kids motive for committing suicide or shooting up a school? It's because no one is protecting them and they

157

are all out of options. A person can only take so much, and once they have taken all that they could take, they mentally snap. Who the hell is going to continuously deal with abuse and bullying? Not Me!!! And if they don't quit fucking with me, I'm going to be the next "Trench Coat Mafia" in this bitch. Yeah I said it, and you probably think I'm bogus for saying it, but that's how I feel. Hurt people...hurt people. And people do and say heartless things not knowing what a person is going through. Then that person has snapped. Take me for example, I was already mentally and emotionally cracked because of that M.A.N., so when Quinton threw those fries in my face, I broke. And I don't regret it neither. If he was bold enough to do that to me, then he was bold enough to accept the consequences behind his actions, no matter what it was. But what I don't understand is why am I being penalized for being provoked? And he gets a smack on the wrist. It's not fair, but I've become immune to being treated unfairly.

They say only the strong survive, but damn how strong

must one be....to live?

    I sat in the office the remainder of the day, mad and hurt. I was a mental and emotional wreck the entire day, and no one noticed.

    Well Myeisha noticed, but she may never talk to me again because I bust her lip.

    Now I was friendless and hopeless.

    I was so miserable. I just wish I had an escape. A place to go to get away from all the pain I was experiencing. I finally understood why people are drug addicts and alcoholics. It's because they need a mental getaway.

    When the bell rang for school to be dismissed, my five-day suspension had officially begun.

OPPORTUNITY

Ever since that M.A.N. broke into my room, I kept a knife in my pillowcase. Cause if he ever tried to break in again, I was going to gut him like a fish.

That Tuesday, I woke up, packed a lunch, and left the house like I normally did for school. I walked around the neighborhood until the library opened. Once the library opened, I stayed there until it was time to pick Kenya up from cheerleading practice.

Once I picked her up, we went to the Community Center.

My first day of suspension went smoothly. However, day two not so much. Because when I left the house it was raining badly. So, roaming the streets was not an option. And neither was staying home with that M.A.N.

So, I got on the bus and pretended to look for my money. When I got to the Red Line train station on 63rd Street, I yelled, "Oh My Goodness I left my purse at the store."

I got off the bus and waited for the driver to pull off. Then I went into the station. I approached the customer service agent and told him that I left my purse on the bus and all my money was in it, so I had no way of getting to my destinations. The agent felt sorry for me and gave me the number to call Chicago Transit Authority (CTA) headquarters to see if someone turned my imaginary purse in.

Not only did he allow me to get on the train for free, he also gave me a token to get home as well. And since I didn't need a token to get home, I saved it for a rainy day.

I rode the train all the way to the end of the line, which was Howard street. Then I got off the train and rode it in the opposite direction, until I got to 95th/Dan Ryan. I rode back and forth until it was time to pick Kenya up.

While on the train I saw people of all ages, colors, and races. I had never seen so many different people in one place.

I was wowed.

The different people wasn't what wowed me, what wowed me was the amount of kindness that was shown. A Caucasian man got up to let a pregnant Hispanic woman sit down. An African woman helped an Arabian woman exit the train with her baby stroller. And an Indian woman gave her seat to an elderly African American man.

All that kindness was new to me.

But don't get me wrong, it wasn't all good. There were teenagers using profanity and disrespecting their elders. I even witnessed a woman get her chain snatched in broad daylight. And I was literally arm reach of the man that did it. As soon as he snatched it, he jumped off the train. I could tell that wasn't his first time robbing anyone, because he timed everything so perfectly.

Several witnesses ran over to comfort the woman. But she was crying hysterically. She just kept saying, "my husband is going to be so mad."

I remember wondering who was he going to be mad at? Her or the person that robbed her? However, I didn't say anything, I just watched her cry over something that could've been replaced. She was acting as if her life was over. I wanted to tell her to shut the hell up. It was just a chain, get another one.

I could see if the necklace was given to her by a deceased family member, then I could sympathize with her, but I doubt if that was the case, because she kept expressing how upset her husband was going to be.

If he's angry at her for being robbed, then she needs to reevaluate her marriage.

The train was crowded during rush hour. But I didn't mind the crowd. I was actually happy to be around something different.

Some people were on their way to work and dressed in their business attire. While others were going from train cart to train cart selling music, movies, and candy. Then there were the beggars. These were the individuals that also went from cart to cart, telling sob stories about their life and begging.

But what amazed me was, people were actually giving them money.

Once we reached downtown, a lot of the commuters exited the train to go to work and school.

I was sitting comfortably in a seat, when the train doors opened. Suddenly loud music started playing. I thought it was the radio, until I glanced out the window, and saw a man sitting on a milk crate, playing the guitar, and singing. The sound of his voice and the way he played that guitar, amazed me. So I got off the train just to listen

to him. As I stood there listening, commuters were walking

pass dropping money in his guitar case. I glanced inside

his case and saw that it was full of money.

Once the crowd died down, he took the money out

of his case and put it inside the leather pouch he wore

around his waist. When he looked up, he saw me staring at

him.

"Do you sing?" He asked.

"No sir," I replied.

"Do you dance?"

"Not really."

"Do you have any talent?"

"Yes, I write."

"Do you write music?"

"I've never tried, but I'm sure I can."

"Well, what do you write?"

"I write short stories and poems. Why do you ask?"

"Trying to figure out why you're staring at me. I thought maybe you wanted to sing."

"No, I was just admiring your talent," I stated.

"Thank you. Are your poems any good?"

"Yes sir," I giggled.

"How often do you write?"

"Daily."

"So if I asked you to recite a poem, will you?"

"I haven't memorized anything that I've written. But I can freestyle something for you."

"Wow…you're able to do that?"

"Yes sir."

The man started playing the guitar. He then looked at me and said, "I'm ready when you are."

Without hesitation I began freestyling to the sound of his guitar.

The look in that man's eyes, the smirk on his face, and the nodding of his head, let me know that he was enjoying my poetry.

In the middle of our performance, a train pulled up, and approximately forty tourist exited. They stopped to listen to us. When I was done performing, I started doing this cool two step dance I learned from grandma. Some of the tourist joined in. After the tourist praised our performance, they put money in that man's guitar case. Although I didn't receive any money, I enjoyed myself, and that's all that mattered to me.

When the tourist left I waited for the next train to arrive. During that time, that man packed his guitar and stood behind me. I slowly eased to the side of him.

"Where are you on your way to?" He asked.

"My grandma's house," I quickly lied.

"Where does your grandmother live?"

"That's top secret information."

The man giggled and said, "top secret huh?"

"Yes sir."

At that moment, the train pulled up. That man entered and I followed behind him. He went to the left to sit, so I went to the right, because all of his questions made me uncomfortable.

Why did he want to know where grandma live? Hell I didn't even know where she lived. But that's not the point. The point was, he was creepy. So I needed to keep my eyes on him.

Once I was seated comfortably, I started eating my lunch. When I looked up, that man was standing over me. My heart skipped a beat and I nervously swallowed a huge piece of my sandwich.

"It was nice meeting you," he said.

"Same here," I lied.

"My stop is coming up, but I wanted to give you something. All females should have one," he said handing me a small pouch and a piece of paper folded into a square.

"What is this?" I asked.

"A note," he replied.

"You put a note in the pouch?"

"No, that's pepper spray," he chuckled.

"Pepper what?" I asked confusedly.

"Some call it mace."

"Aw the self-defense spray?"

"Yes, a pretty girl like yourself don't need to be out here unprotected."

"Thank you sir."

"All my friends call me Hendrix," he said.

"Like the guitarist Jimi Hendrix?" I asked.

"You got it little lady. This is my stop. Enjoy the rest of your day."

"Enjoy your day as well Mr. Hendrix, and thanks for the pepper spray."

"Anytime little lady," he said as he exited the train.

When he got off the train I unfolded the piece of paper. Inside the paper was twenty-seven dollars. I was shocked, yet happy.

On the paper Mr. Hendrix wrote:

"Your talent is God's gift to you. What you do with it is your gift back to God. Don't lose your talent, because you are truly bless. Here is your half of what was earned today. Take care, be safe, and don't be afraid to use your pepper spray."

~Hendrix

I put the money in my left pocket, the pepper spray in my right, and the letter in my backpack, because I wanted to always remember Mr. Hendrix words.

The very next morning I took my entire twenty-seven dollars and bought snacks from the neighborhood store.

I filled my backpack with the goodies I purchased.

I went to the train station, got on the crowded train, and yelled, "Get Your Chips, Candy, Juice, and Water Here!"

I doubled my profit by charging twice as much as I paid, but unbeknownst to me, a quarter bag of chips downtown was $1. So people were gladly paying .50 cents.

A lot of the high school and college students purchased the chips, candy, and juice. The business men and women only purchased water.

One lady whispered, "you should consider selling fruit."

"I'll see what I can do ma'am," I replied.

By the time I got to the third cart, I was completely sold out. So I patiently waited for the business men and women to arrive to their destination, so that I could eat my lunch.

Riding back and forth from the Northside of Chicago to the Southside of Chicago was very entertaining for me. I'm not sure why, it just was.

Once I got home from the Community Center, I cut a small hole in the bottom of my teddy bear and put my money inside of it.

It was Friday and day four of my suspension. I left home, caught the bus to the local grocery store, and purchased a CTA transfer.

As I walked in each aisle I noticed that the items I purchased from the neighborhood store, were cheaper at the grocery store. That allowed me to make a bigger profit and purchase more products.

I grabbed a shopping cart and filled it with chips, candy, juice, water, a bag of oranges, a bag of apples, grapes, and a cluster of bananas. I then grabbed a hand full of plastic produce bags from the produce section. Once I paid for everything, I sat in the parking lot, separated all the fruit, and put them in individual produce bags. Each fruit bag contained an orange, a banana, an apple, and a small cluster of grapes. I tied the produce bags into a knot and carried them in the thermal bag I purchased from the grocery store.

I packed all the other snacks and beverages in my backpack.

I then took the bus to the train station, and immediately began selling the items. Surprisingly my $2 fruit bags were the first to go. The lady that suggested I sell fruit, purchased two bags and gave me a dollar tip.

Once again I sold out of everything before I got to the last few carts.

At the rate I was going, I wasn't looking forward to going back to school.

Like the previous days, I waited until the train was empty and ate my lunch.

I continued to ride the train, until it was time to pick Kenya up.

I was anxiously waiting for the weekend to pass, so I could get back to business.

Monday finally arrived and it was the last day of my suspension. I went to Stanley's bedroom and got his huge duffle bag. I caught the bus to the grocery store and stocked up on products.

That day was better than all the rest because I had more money and more bags to carry items in. I had my backpack, a duffle bag, and the thermal bag. I bought as much as I could to filled each bag. Carrying all of those bags on the bus and train was tedious, but I made it work.

Once I got on the train people recognized me right away. They approached me immediately.

I made more money than I've ever experienced, and I loved it.

One man purchased $35 worth of products. He gave me seven $5 bills. I quickly counted the money, put it in my jacket pocket, zipped it closed, and continued serving my other customers.

I successfully sold everything. However, I was so focused on making money that I forgot to pack a lunch.

I folded Stanley's duffle bag and put it in my backpack. The thermal bag couldn't fit in my book bag, so I had to carry it.

I wanted to wait until I got back to the Southside of Chicago to get something to eat, because that was the part of town I was familiar with. However, I was a long way from the Southside.

I hadn't eaten the entire day, and I was starving. So I got off the train at a random stop to find the nearest restaurant.

Once I exited the train I smelled food. There were several restaurants in the area, but the first thing I noticed when I exited the train station, was a sign that read, *"Oscar's Dog House Has The Best Chicago Style Hotdogs in The City."*

I've never had a Chicago style hotdog, so I went there.

On my way inside the restaurant I walked passed a homeless man.

"Hello," he greeted.

"Hi," I replied.

"Are you going in there?" He asked pointing to Oscar's Dog House Restaurant.

"Yes."

"If you have any leftovers, may you please think about me? I haven't eaten in over forty-eight hours and I am really hungry."

His desperation frightened me. I put my hand in my pocket and grabbed my mace, because if that man would have come any closer I would have sprayed him with no hesitation.

I had never seen anyone beg for scraps before.

I honestly didn't believe him, and I felt that he had an ulterior motive, so I shook my head and kept walking.

However, I felt something in my gut. True enough I was hungry, but it wasn't a hunger pain. It was a sympathetic feeling. But why was I feeling like that? Why was I sympathizing with a man I didn't know?

Furthermore, I hated men. That M.A.N. made me hate men. And unfortunately, that homeless individual was a man.

Nevertheless, I thought about my situation. When people ignored my cries for help, I was upset and hurt. So why was I ignoring his?

But I was a girl and he was a man. I'm sure a million and one people walk pass him daily. Why didn't he ask them for scraps? Why did he have to ask me?

At that moment I remembered something grandma told me, ***"you have not lived today until you have done something for someone who can never repay you."***

I said to myself, *"this dumb heart of mine!"*

I wanted to ignore that man so bad, Lord knows I did, but I just put my head down and said, "Heavenly Father, if I was hungry I would want someone to feed me. You blessed me with the means to help this man, so I will do so. But Father please, please don't let this man be a crazy killer."

I took a deep breath, and approached the man with my hand still in my pocket holding on to my pepper spray.

"Sir," I said.

He looked at me and replied, "yes."

"I apologize for ignoring you earlier."

"It's okay, you're not the first to ignore me, but you are the first to apologize."

"May I please buy you lunch?" I asked.

"You don't have to do that. I would happily take your leftovers."

"My leftovers? You mean the scraps I don't eat?"

"Yes," he replied.

"Oh no sir, I would do no such thing. You are not a dog; therefore, I will not treat you as one."

That man's eyes watered, but he didn't drop a tear.

"I know, but you don't know me. And some people think I'm a mass murderer because I live on the street."

My eyes got big as I took my hands off my pepper spray.

"Wow people and their imagination. Well mister I'll buy you lunch. You can even sit with me while we wait for our meal to be prepared."

"But I'm dirty," he said shamefully.

"Well that's why God invented soap and water. I'm sure the restaurant has a bathroom, just wash your face and hands before you eat."

"My name is Ralph by the way," he said.

"Mines is Destiny."

"Nice to meet you Destiny."

Mr. Ralph had to walk on the side of me, because I didn't trust any man to walk behind me. It may be weird to some, but the reality was…I was still battling with abuse issues. I was working through them though. Sitting with a male stranger and having lunch, was a huge step for me. But you better believe, I had my pepper spray very close.

When Mr. Ralph and I walked in Oscar's Dog House restaurant, the manager went ballistic. He was yelling at Mr. Ralph, and treating him rudely. He told him that he was not welcome in their establishment. He kept calling him a dirty worthless bum. He even told Mr. Ralph

to kill himself because he was a disgrace to the human race.

His words cut me deeply, because I knew how it felt

to be criticized and I knew how it felt to want to commit

suicide. Hell I knew how it felt to attempt suicide because

of abuse and bullying. So to hear a person tell another

human being that they need to end their life, angered me.

But I kept my composure, and kindly said, "sir he is with

me!"

The manager was so busy degrading Mr. Ralph that

he didn't hear me.

The manager grabbed a broom and began

threatening him, telling him to get out because he was

running customers away. Mr. Ralph tried to explain but the

manager wouldn't listen. He just continued threatening

him.

"Sir, he is with me!" I yelled again, holding up a

twenty-dollar bill.

The manager stopped swinging the broom and told Mr. Ralph he could get his food to go. Mr. Ralph was so happy to have a meal that he politely said, "Okay."

I was enraged and could no longer keep my composure.

"No its not okay for him to treat you that way."

I then looked at the manager and said, "who the hell do you think you are telling someone to kill themselves? You think your life is so secure, no honey, you are two paychecks away from being in any unfortunate situation. So you better count your blessings and pray that you never lose your job, cause the hand you bite today, may be the one you need to feed you tomorrow. You evil bastard!"

I then looked at Mr. Ralph and said, "Let's Go!"

"It's okay, I'll take my food to go Destiny," Mr. Ralph said.

"I wish I would spend my money in this raggedy place."

Mr. Ralph put his head down and quickly left the restaurant.

I looked at the manager one last time, rolled my eyes, and left.

When I exited the restaurant Mr. Ralph was half way down the street.

"Mr. Ralph!" I called.

When he turned around I said, "where are you going?"

"To the park," he answered in a sad voice.

"I thought you were having lunch with me?"

"But you said you're not spending your money there."

"And I meant that. That's why we're going to the Pizzeria up the street."

Mr. Ralph lit up like a Christmas tree when he realized I was still going to buy him lunch.

As we walked to the Pizzeria he said, "Thank you Destiny for defending me."

"No need to thank me. He had no right to treat you that way. He is a bully and I hate bullies."

Once we got to the Pizzeria. People were staring at us and whispering.

"Maybe I should wait outside until the pizza is ready," Mr. Ralph said.

"You will do no such thing. *My grandma said, "every time you judge someone, you reveal a part of yourself that needs healing."* You are a paying customer. And if they have a problem with you being here, then they can leave. Cause at the end of the day we are all human. We breathe, we eat, we cry, we laugh, we love, and we hate, so who are they to judge you?"

"I am not worried about them judging me, I'm worried about embarrassing you."

I snickered and said, "the less you worry, the less complicated life becomes."

At that moment the hostess greeted us, handed us menus, walked us to a table, and gave us the name of our server.

Once we were seated Mr. Ralph went to the bathroom and washed his face and hands. When he returned, I asked, "do you know what you're going to order?"

"I'll have what you're having," he said.

"I want you to order what you want. Matter of fact I want you to order yourself the largest pizza they have. And add extra cheese, veggies, meat, or whatever else you desire. Today I want Mr. Ralph to get something that Mr. Ralph wants."

"I'm just worried about my meal being too expensive. Because you didn't have to…."

I interrupted and giggled, "there you go worrying again. Living in worry, invites death in a hurry."

Mr. Ralph laughed and then looked at the menu once more.

The waitress walked to our table, "my name is Wendy and I'll be your server. Can I start you off with something to drink?"

"Yes, may I have a glass of water with lemon and a glass of lemonade," I said.

"And for you sir?" Wendy asked.

"I'll have water with lemon as well," Mr. Ralph replied.

"Just water? How about Pepsi, Mount Dew, 7UP, or lemonade?" I asked.

"I don't drink soda and I haven't had lemonade in years."

I looked at Wendy and said, "make that two glasses of water with lemon and a pitcher of lemonade."

"Do you need more time to order?" Wendy asked.

"Yes, but can you tell me more about the appetizer sampler."

"The appetizer sampler comes with mozzarella sticks, wings with your choice of dipping sauce, and fried ravioli," Wendy explained.

"Okay we will take that."

"Great, well let me get your appetizers started and bring you your drinks. I'll be back to take your order shortly."

"Thank you," I said.

When Wendy left Mr. Ralph asked, "what is fried ravioli?"

"I don't know, but we're about to find out. Why don't you drink soda?"

"It's a long story."

When Wendy returned with our drinks I ordered a small sausage and cheese deep dish pizza. And Mr. Ralph ordered an extra-large thin crust supreme pizza.

When the appetizers came Mr. Ralph bowed his head and mumbled.

I assumed he was saying grace.

The fried ravioli turned out to be quite delicious.

While we were eating Mr. Ralph said, "thank you for everything."

"You're welcome! How do you like the lemonade?"

"It's pretty good," he answered.

"Well it's only okay to me, because my grandma makes the best homemade lemonade in the world."

"Does she?"

"Yes and sometimes she adds strawberries, oranges, and limes."

"That sounds good. Can she cook?"

"Can she? Man she is the best cook ever. And her peach cobbler is to die for."

"Where is your grandmother now?"

Mr. Ralph words made me sad, because I didn't know where grandma was. But I couldn't let him know I was sad so I quickly replied, "aw she's at home, I'm going to see her when I leave here."

"Did I say something wrong?" Mr. Ralph asked.

"No, why did you ask that?" I said inserting a fraudulent smile.

"Because your facial expression and body language changed."

"Oh no you're fine," I said trying to convince him that I was okay.

Mr. Ralph changed the subject by asking, "are you some type of angel or something?"

"No sir, not even close," I giggled.

"People aren't blessing people the way you have blessed me," he said.

"Well my **grandma said, treat people the way you want to be treated, and talk to people the way you want to be talked to, because respect is earned not given.**"

"So Destiny if you don't mind, can you please tell me about yourself."

"All I can tell you is; I'm surviving the best way I know how."

"I'm surviving as well, and I am barely doing that," he said.

"I know what you mean," I said.

"Do you really?" He asked.

"Yes I really do."

"How can a young lovely girl like yourself say such a thing."

"Please don't call me lovely, that word makes my skin crawl."

"Lovely makes your skin crawl?" He asked confusedly.

"Yes sir."

"Why is that?"

"I don't want to talk about it."

"Okay, I'll respect your wishes," he said.

"So what's your story? Are you a drug addict or an alcoholic?" I asked.

"Neither. I've never done drugs and when I drank in the past, it was always occasionally."

"I thought the only people that were homeless were drug addicts and alcoholics."

"I think a lot of people are ignorant when it comes to that matter, and that's why they look down on me because they feel I put myself in this situation. Which technically I did."

"What do you mean by technically?"

"I was ungrateful and took my life for granted."

"I don't understand."

"Destiny rock bottom will teach you lessons that mountain tops never will."

"I still don't understand," I said.

"It's a long story."

"Well we have time, the waitress said the pizza will take at least thirty minutes. So if you're willing to talk, I'm willing to listen."

"I wasn't always poor. I was actually quite wealthy. I traveled many countries and states. I drove the most expensive cars and I even had the biggest house in the neighborhood. Eight bedrooms, two kitchens, theater room, pool, exercise room, and six bathrooms. I had it all. My wife and I entertained at our house quite often."

"You were married?" I asked.

"Yes and she was beautiful inside and out. If only I would have cherished the gift God gave me, she would probably still be here today."

"Did she leave you?"

"Yes, she unwillingly left me," he said with sadness in his eyes.

"I'm confused. How do you unwillingly leave someone?"

"Okay, let me start from the beginning. I was the Chief Operating Officer (COO), at a billion-dollar company. I was making six figures a year. During that time, I was boastful, egotistical, and selfish. I would walk pass a homeless person and tell them to get a job. Call them lazy and pathetic.

The sad thing was, my wallet would be full of one hundred dollar bills, and I wouldn't give them a quarter.

I constantly cheated on my beautiful wife, Sophia. Spoiling other women by paying their bills, giving them money, and buying them expensive gifts.

Sophia caught me numerous times and never left me nor stopped loving me.

I honestly thought she stayed because of the money.

Our company made a bad investment, and we lost millions of dollars. The company was forced to file bankruptcy and closed shortly after. Which caused all the employees to lose their jobs. I was able to survive on my savings and pension. But that was short lived because I had grown accustomed to living a certain lifestyle.

I applied for other jobs and got hired. But when they weren't willing to pay what I made at my old job, I declined their offer. I was so sure that I would find another job making six figures, but I didn't. And those jobs I turned down in the past, I was now calling and begging to be rehired. However, the positions were already filled.

I was so busy trying to hold on to the house and vehicles I could no longer afford, that I got deeper and deeper in debt.

Our health and life insurance expired because I stopped paying the bills.

Sophia never had to work in the past because I was so wealthy. But while I was out turning down jobs, she was submitting applications.

When I asked her why was she looking for a job, she said, *"what kind of wife would I be if I sat back and waited for things to happen?"*

Any other woman would have left me when the money dried up. But not her. She was actually the opposite of me. She was loyal and didn't care about the expensive vehicles, the house, or the money. All she wanted was a healthy child and my unconditional love.

I officially hit rock bottom when I started working as a stock boy at a warehouse. I wasn't comfortable working a factory job. My jobs were always corporate friendly. So to go from wearing suits to wearing steel toe boots, goggles, gloves, dirty jeans, and long sleeve shirts, was depressing. But I had no choice, because I lost everything.

We had to sell every expensive thing we owned. Including our wedding rings.

All those friends I once had, disappeared. And not one of my family members allowed us to live with them.

Sophia could've lived with her family, but I wasn't welcomed. They didn't like me, and I don't blame them, because I mistreated everyone.

But she refused to leave me without a place to stay.

Can you believe she stayed even after I was so disloyal and disrespectful?

Everyone turned their backs on me. Everyone except Sophia. But I was so mad at what my life had become that I took it out on her. And no matter how much I yelled or degraded her, she always tried to cheer me up and tell me that our situation was temporary. She often said, *"the rain doesn't last forever, when the storm ends there will be a pot of goal at the end of the rainbow waiting for us."* I couldn't see what she saw. I couldn't see the pot of gold waiting for us at the end of the rainbow. And I couldn't understand why she was so positive. I was mad as hell and I wanted her to be mad to. We went from living in a baby mansion, to living in a studio apartment.

I was so bitter and miserable that I became verbally and mentally abusive. Sophia didn't deserve that. She packed my lunch every morning and every night I came home to a hot meal and a clean house.

Although she was tired from work, she still made sure I was okay. But I didn't appreciate it, I just complained and found reasons to yell.

I remember the last lunch Sophia packed for me. It was a Thursday morning. We were both getting ready for work. At the time we had an old raggedy car. I drove to work and made her take public transportation. I had enough time to drop her off at work, but I didn't. Because I was too darn selfish. Nevertheless, I grabbed my lunch and left out the door. I didn't kiss my wife, or tell her goodbye or I loved her.

When I got to work I opened my lunch bag and there was a turkey sandwich on wheat with mayo lettuce and tomato, a bag of chips, some homemade cookies, cherries, an apple, a cold bottle of water, a juice, and a note that read, *"Have a great day. I love you."*

Do you know I called her at work and complained about not having enough mayo on my sandwich? Instead of her yelling back at me for being ungrateful, she apologized.

Later that day I got a call. Sophia had a seizure at work. I thought they called the wrong number because, she never had a seizure before. I left work and rushed to the hospital. When I got there she was getting a computerized axial tomography (CAT) scan.

When I finally saw her she looked at me, smiled, and said, "*are you okay?*" Here she was lying in a hospital bed and she was worried about me being okay. I gave her a hug and kiss. Several doctors walked in and closed the door. I knew something wasn't right so I slowly stood up and asked what's wrong. One of the doctors explained that my wife had cancer. The reason she had a seizure was because there was a large tumor on her brain.

"What does that mean, what does that mean!" I yelled.

The doctor said that the only thing they could do is make her transition as comfortable as possible. I held my wife tightly, as we both cried. It wasn't until that moment that I realized how blessed I was to have her in my life. The moment I began to truly cherish her, was when I realized I was about to lose her. I never thought she would leave me. But God took her from me, because I took her for granted for so many years.

Do you know what her last words to me were?"

"No, what were they?" I asked.

"Thank you for not leaving me when I needed you the most. I love you."

Then she asked me to go to the vendor machine to get her a Pepsi. She loved Pepsi.

I gave her a kiss, told her I love her, she told me she loved me, I told her I will be right back. But when I came back the doctors and nurses wouldn't let me enter the room. Sophia knew she was about to make her transition, but she didn't want me to see her take her last breath. I regret ever leaving her side to get that freaking Pepsi.

To this day I refuse to drink any brand of soda, pop.

I had to have Sophia cremated because of my selfish decisions. We didn't have life insurance, because I was so worried about the materialistic things, that I didn't make sure my wife was okay. I was mad at myself for being so ornery and selfish.

I miss her every single day. She taught me how to be thankful for the small things in life, she showed me what true love was, she showed me the true definition of loyalty, and I showed her nothing.

When she died a big piece of my heart died with her. I couldn't sleep, I couldn't eat, I was so lost. I was all alone in the world with no one and nothing.

I was fired from the factory job, and evicted from our apartment. I lived in my car until it was impounded for expired tags. I then went to a shelter, but they only let me stay there overnight and put me and the rest of the guys out during the day. They would tell us to find a job, but we had no means of transportation or communication? The shelter didn't want to help us for real, they just pretended so that they could continue getting funding from the government. All we were doing as homeless men was wasting our lives away, and our presence was keeping the contributions for the shelter rolling in.

When I voiced my opinion about not being helped properly, they banned me from the shelter. That's how I ended up on the street. I regret ever saying anything because at least they fed me, I was able to shower, and sleep in a bed.

I haven't slept in a bed in years."

"Where do you sleep now?" I asked.

"Mainly on the park bench. But the police sometimes harass me."

"What do you do then?"

"I read. I have three books that I read over and over again. They are pretty good books so I don't mind."

"Did you and Ms. Sophia have children?"

"Yes and no."

"What does that mean?"

"We tried to have children but her body wasn't strong enough. I spent thousands of dollars on doctors, but she never had a successful pregnancy. She was able to get pregnant but she wasn't able to hold a baby full term."

"Aw, that's so sad."

"It was very sad watching my wife lose twelve babies. But it was even sadder having to tell her I got another woman pregnant."

"You did what?"

"Yes one of the women I cheated with, became pregnant."

"How did you let that happen?"

"Being dumb and selfish. I was messing with a young lady for months. I admit I spoiled her, bought her things, took her to fancy restaurants. I even took her on a business trip with me. I treated her like she had never been treated before.

I didn't think it was a big deal because she knew I was married. But she fell in love with me and wanted me to divorce Sophia, so we could be together.

One day she saw Sophia at the mall, and her and her girlfriends tried to attack my wife. Thank goodness security was there to stop them. I blamed myself for that incident because Bella's mother should have never known who Sophia was. Sadly, men have a tendency of treating the side chick like the main chick and the main chick like the side chick. That was one of the mistakes I made. Once I found out her and her friends tried to harm Sophia I left her alone. She called me weeks later and told me she was pregnant. I thought it was a cry for attention or a way to get more money from me. So I gave her some money and told her to get an abortion. I never heard from her again. Until I received a court order in the mail for child support. So I requested a DNA test. And it came back that the baby girl was mine."

"How did Ms. Sophia feel?"

"She was so heartbroken because another woman gave me something she couldn't. She cried for days and there wasn't anything I could do to stop her tears.

Then one morning she woke up and said, *"I'm ready to meet your daughter, it's not her fault her mother is a Jezebel and her father is a selfish jackass."*

So I called Bella's mother and asked can I come get her for the weekend. She allowed me to.

When I went to pick up Bella, her mother was having a house party. People were smoking cigarettes and marijuana. There were empty liquor bottles everywhere. I grabbed my two-month old baby off a dirty mattress and wrapped her in a towel. All she had on was a t-shirt and a dirty diaper. I had to drive home with her in my arms praying I didn't get pulled over by the police.

When I got home I handed her to my wife. Sophia was so upset. She told me we had to go to the store immediately. I drove while Sophia held Bella in the backseat. My daughter was crying uncontrollably.

Once we got to the store Sophia went in and I stayed in the car with Bella.

Sophia bought her a sleeper, baby wipes, a blanket, nursery water, formula, a pack of diapers, and disposable bottles.

She then came back to the car and made Bella a bottle.

Once my baby got her bottle, she stopped crying.

Sophia then cleaned Bella with baby wipes. As she cleaned Bella she noticed that she had a really bad diaper rash. She then put her on the sleeper and wrapped her in a blanket. We went back in the store and bought Bella some clothes, bibs, diaper rash cream, baby wash, baby lotion, a stroller, a car seat, a baby crib, and any and everything else a baby needed.

That night Sophia fell asleep with Bella in her arms."

"Your daughter's name is Bella?" I asked.

"Yes, but Sophia called her, *"Beautiful Blessing."*

"Why did she call her that? Bella was a mistake not a blessing."

"Because Sophia prayed for a child. One day Sophia looked into Bella's eyes and said, *this is our "Beautiful Blessing." God's plan is always the best. Sometimes the process is painful and hard. But God is in control and He has the perfect plan for our lives."*

Sophia found beauty and blessings in everything. So when Bella's mother started neglecting her, she felt that it was our responsibility to save Bella. So we filed for custody."

"Was Bella's mom really that bad?"

"She was young and wasn't mentally prepared to be a mother. She still wanted to live her life like she did before Bella was born.

Sophia asked Bella's mother can she stay with us until she get on her feet, but she wasn't willing to give us Bella because my daughter was her meal ticket. I was paying child support so if she gave us Bella, I would no longer have to pay.

Sophia didn't care about the money so she told Bella's mother if she allowed Bella to live with us, we would still pay her every month. Her mother agreed, so we dropped the court case when Bella moved in with us. And as my wife promised every month a check was in the mail.

Once Bella moved in with us, we legally changed her name to Bella Eliana Pryor. My wife named her that because Bella means *"beautiful"* and Eliana means *"My God has answered."* My wife truly believed Bella was her answered prayer."

"What was Bella's name before you changed it?"

"Alize," Mr. Ralph answered.

I giggled and said, "you had an awesome wife. Not only did she forgive you for cheating, she also helped you raise the baby that you conceived through adultery. And paid the other woman monthly."

"Sophia was very awesome. She never mistreated Bella because of my mistakes. She loved Bella and Bella loved her.

Bella's biological mother stopped calling and coming around, so Sophia was the only mother she knew.

Bella moved in with us when she was 4 months old. We experienced all her special moments. Her first steps, her first teeth, and her first words.

Sophia toilet trained her, taught her how to read, her colors, her letters, her numbers, and how to pray.

"So what happened to Bella?"

"When I lost my job I stopped paying Bella's mother. And one day she unexpectedly showed up at our house with the police."

"What happened then?"

"They took my baby and gave her to her biological mother."

"How could they do that if she lived with you guys," I asked.

"Bella's mother was receiving government assistance for her, so the police said she had documents proving she was the custodial parent."

"But that wasn't true. And how was she getting government assistance for Bella, if she lived with you?" I questioned.

"Because she was receiving it under Bella's old name. We showed the policemen the new birth certificate and the name change documents, but they told us it was out of their control and if we wanted her back we needed to go through the courts.

Watching the police take Bella out of Sophia's arms, and watching them both break down emotionally crushed me. Have you ever seen the movie, "The Color Purple?"

"That's my favorite movie," I said.

"Do you remember the scene when Mister took Nettie from Celie. And they were holding on to one another for dear life?"

"I do, because it made me cry when Nettie told Celie, *"nothing but death can keep me from it."*

"Yep, now picture a wife and child holding on to one another for dear life, crying, screaming, begging, and pleading to stay with one another. That shattered me because I was their protector and I couldn't protect them."

A few tears fell from Mr. Ralph's eyes. He took a napkin and wiped his face.

"I'm sorry, I didn't mean to get emotional."

"It's okay," I said.

He then continued, "at one point Bella broke away from the police and ran into Sophia's arms and begged her not to let them take her, but it wasn't anything we could do. Bella's biological mother forcefully snatched Bella by the arm and yelled, "I AM YOUR MOTHER." Sophia pushed Bella's mom and was ready to fight. That was shocking to me because Sophia wasn't aggressive or violent, but she was willing to fight for her *"Beautiful Blessing."* But the police grabbed Sophia and told Bella's mother to leave. I grabbed my wife from the police. I was yelling at them, for not protecting my daughter. They threatened to lock me up if I didn't calm down, so Sophia and I went in the house.

That was the last time we saw Bella. Sophia was devastated because she lost yet another child. And this time was worst then all the miscarriages combined because my wife and daughter had a bond. My wife cried every night for two months, because she missed her, *"Beautiful Blessing."*

"Have you tried to find Bella since then?"

"Yes, but her mother moved away, and changed her phone number. We went to court for custody, but her mother never attended any of the court dates.

There was a warrant for her arrest, but when I could no longer afford to pay the lawyers, our case eventually closed."

"Once the case closed did you stopped looking for her?" I asked.

"Yes, because I was embarrassed at what my life had become. I would love to see her, but I am too ashamed to search for her now. Because no daughter should ever see her father this way. Besides I wouldn't know where to begin to look for her. "

Hearing Mr. Ralph story made my heart bleed. You can never judge a book by its cover. Cause you never know what's inside, until you start exploring for yourself.

At that moment Wendy brought out our pizza.

"Please bow your head," Mr. Ralph said.

"For what?"

"To give thanks."

"You still thank God?" I asked.

"Yes ma'am. Each and every day."

"But He took away your job, your house, your wife, and your daughter."

"God didn't do that; my karma did that. Destiny I needed to be humbled. I never thanked God when I had my good job, my enormous house, my gorgeous wife, and my beautiful daughter. I took advantage of everything I had. I criticized others for not being as successful as I was. Or for not having as much knowledge as I had. I had parties at my house to secretly boast.

Sophia was taken away because I didn't cherish her. She deserved so much more than what I gave her, but no matter what I did, she was never going to leave me. So God took her through those pearly gates, where she is forever loved and cherished."

I now understood what grandma meant when she told mom, *"never get too cocky or too big headed about yourself. Enjoy every blessing that God is allowing you to have and do, because as easy as He gave it to you He can quickly take it away. You must be humble and stay humble."*

I bowed my head as Mr. Ralph began to pray.

"For the food in a world where many walk in hunger, for faith in a world where many walk in fear, for friends in a world where many walk alone, and for blessings that comes in the form of strangers. We give You thanks, O'Lord. Amen."

"Amen," I repeated.

"Who taught you that prayer?" I asked.

Mr. Ralph laughed and said, "that's just something I say often. No one taught me, it's just what I feel in my heart."

"May you please teach me that specific prayer?" I asked.

"Sure," he said as he recited it and I repeated after him.

What do you say to a man that has endured so much? And true enough he admits that his unfortunateness was caused by his selfishness, ungratefulness, and arrogance.

But dang, will he ever be done paying back that debt called "karma?"

"Do you have a plan?" I asked.

"What do you mean by plan?"

"Do you plan on dying a homeless man?"

"Of course not," Mr. Ralph replied.

"So how do you plan on changing your situation?"

"That's a great question."

"Am I being too nosey?"

"No Destiny it's just a question."

"So, what are your plans to get back on your feet?"

"I have no plans. I would love to get a job but…"

"But what?"

"No one is going to hire me, because I'm a bum."

"Why are you referring to yourself as a bum?"

"It's my reality Destiny," Mr. Ralph said holding his head down in shame.

"Is that how you view yourself or are you allowing the words of others to influence what you think about yourself? Because my **grandma said, *"it's not what they call you, it's what you answer to."***

"Your grandmother sounds like a smart woman."

"She is the smartest and greatest woman I know. But don't change the subject."

"I wasn't trying to change the subject. To answer your question, all I need is an opportunity."

"What do you mean by opportunity?"

"A chance. If someone would just gamble on me, I promise not to disappoint them and I promise to never take life for granted again."

"If my grandma was here do you know what advice she would give you?"

"No, what?"

"She would say, ***"honey to change your life, you have to change yourself. To change yourself, you have to change your mindset. You are not a bum, you're just a*** *man that is in his season of test. You can't have a*

testimony without first having a test."

Mr. Ralph took a bite of his pizza, looked up at me with glossy eyes, and said, "are you sure that's what your grandmother would say? Or is that coming from you?"

"Well I may have paraphrased a little, but she would have definitely said something along those lines."

Mr. Ralph didn't say anything, he just nodded his head and continued eating his pizza.

"How does it taste?" I asked

"It's heavenly," he uttered as he rose his head and stared at a specific spot with fear in his eyes.

I looked in the direction he was staring at.

Wendy and the manager were both standing at our table.

"I'll leave," Mr. Ralph stuttered.

"You don't have to leave sir. I'm just making sure everything was to your liking, and if there was anything else you needed," the manager said.

"Everything is great, thanks for asking," I replied.

The manager then smiled and walked away.

Mr. Ralph exhaled a sigh of relief.

"Are you okay?" I asked.

"Yes," he answered.

When we were done eating I asked Wendy for the bill. She sat what I thought was the bill on the table. When I turned the receipt over, it was a note that said, *"**Please See Manager For Further Details!**"*

I was so afraid. I thought he was going to call the police, because I was supposed to be in school. But I knew I couldn't leave, so I nervously walked to the register.

"Hello sir. The waitress gave me this," I said handing him the note.

"What is your name?"

"Why?" I asked.

"I would like to know the name of the young lady that opened my heart."

"I'm sorry, but I don't understand sir."

"Please allow me to explain. I see that man every day."

"Who Mr. Ralph?"

"Is that his name?"

"Yes sir."

"I walk pass Mr. Ralph every day I come to work. There were even times I stepped over him to get to work. And it never crossed my mind to feed him. Do you know we throw food away daily?"

"You throw food in the garbage?"

"Yes."

"But why?"

"According to United States Department of Agriculture (USDA) restaurants must discard any perishable foods left out at room temperature after a certain number of hours."

"So why don't you give it to customers before those hours expire?"

"Then we will lose paying customers. Because everyone will come in expecting free pizza."

"So instead of giving it away, you throw it away?" I asked confusedly.

"I'm afraid so."

"That's pretty dumb."

"I agree, but what I was getting at was, I could have given Mr. Ralph one of those pizzas. I feel so bad. Because here you are a child probably spending your allowance to feed a man that I've ignored countlessly."

"Well there is always tomorrow, and the next day, and the day after that."

"I just wanted to tell you thank you for opening my eyes and heart."

"Your welcome. May I have the receipt because I have to leave, my grandmother is waiting for me," I lied.

The manager handed me a receipt and in big letters "PAID" was written across the top. I looked at him confused.

He smiled and said, "your meal and tip is on me."

"Wait! What do I have to do for this free meal?" I questioned.

"Nothing, this is my gift to you, for showing me that there are still some good people in the world."

"Thank you sir," I said smiling from ear to ear.

"The name is Derrick," he said extending his hand out to shake mine.

I shook his hand and went back to the table to get my backpack and thermal bag.

"Wendy separated our food," Mr. Ralph said.

I took all the boxes of food off the table and put it in the thermal bag and handed the entire bag to Mr. Ralph.

"This will help you keep your food fresh," I said.

"Thank you! May I hug you?" He asked.

"No sir, just fist bump me," I said holding out my fist.

I'm sure Mr. Ralph thought I didn't want to hug him because he was dirty. But I didn't hug him because he was a man. And I didn't want, or need any man touching me affectionately.

Before I left the Pizzeria, I thanked Mr. Derrick once again for his kindness.

I then headed to the train station.

On my way to the train I walked passed a motel. I was scratching my head, because I didn't recall walking pass it on my way to Oscar's Dog House or The Pizzeria.

I went inside to inquire prices, so I could get Mr. Ralph a room for the night since I didn't have to pay for our food.

The inside of the motel wasn't the best looking place. It reeked of cigarettes smoke, funk, and liquor. And the desk clerk sat behind bullet proof glass. I walked to the clerk and asked how much to rent a room. He explained that I could purchase a room for four hours, six hours, eight hours, or the entire day.

As he was explaining the prices, a woman walked in wearing a short skirt, a pink wig, high heel boots, and a bra. She was holding an older man's arm. The man looked at me and winked.

I instantly put my hand on my pepper spray as I wrinkled my nose in disgust.

"May I see a room," I asked the clerk.

"Yes meet me in the hallway," he replied.

Once we got in the hallway he took me to room 29. The room wasn't as bad as I thought. It had a mini refrigerator, a microwave, a bed, bathroom, and television. I went in the bathroom and turned the water on to see if it worked. Then I turned on the television. The clerk explained that they only had basic cable.

I snickered because we didn't have any cable at my house.

"This is one of the best rooms we have. Not all rooms have refrigerators and microwaves. But I'm sure you will be comfortable here," he said.

"The room isn't for me."

"It's not?" The desk clerk asked.

"No, it's for my uncle. He lost his home, and tomorrow is his birthday. So as a gift I wanted to get him a room," I lied.

"Aw man that's sad."

"Yeah it is, he needs a job but no one is willing to hire him because he's homeless. He wants to work, but no one will give him the opportunity to prove himself."

"Wow…I know what that feels like."

"You do?" I asked shockingly.

"Yes I was homeless at one point in my life," the desk clerk said.

"How did you turn your life around?" I asked.

"Meet me at the front desk," he said.

Once I got to the front, the desk clerk handed me a sheet of paper.

"This is the address and phone number to an Outreach Center that helped me. Every Sunday they give out hot meals, free haircuts, and clothes. If your uncle can find a way there, they will give him transportation back to his destination."

"Thank you very much, I'll give him this information," I said as I unzipped my jacket pocket, stuffed the piece of paper inside, and zipped it back up.

"Also here is a care package for him. We usually sell these for $5, but since it's his birthday, this will be my gift to him."

The care package contained soap, toothbrush, toothpaste, mouthwash, socks, gum, hand sanitizer, deodorant, and chap stick.

Then randomly the clerk asked, "do you have a dollar?"

I assumed he was charging me for the care package.

But I was confused because he told me it was free?

Nevertheless, I went into my pocket, pulled out a dollar, and handed it to him. He then handed me a key with the number 29 on it.

"What is this?"

"You wanted to rent a room right?"

"Oh yes," I said as I dug in my pants pocket for the money.

"What are you doing?" He asked.

"Paying you for the room," I slowly replied.

"You've already paid."

"When?"

"You just handed me your money, did you forget?"

"I only gave you a dollar," I replied trying to figure out what he was talking about.

"Young lady a dollar and a big heart is all you need."

"I'm confused," I replied.

"A beautiful heart can bring things in your life that all the money in the world can't obtain. You told me your uncle needed an opportunity. Someone blessed me with one, so I am going to pay it forward. I am going to give your uncle room 29 for 10 days. Now what he does with the next ten days of his life, is up to him."

My eyes began to water and I couldn't understand why. Why was I so happy for Mr. Ralph? Why did him getting that room make me emotional?

I thanked the clerk and ran out the motel door. I went searching for Mr. Ralph.

I couldn't wait to tell him the good news.

I found him in the park, on the bench, reading, with the thermal bag on his lap.

"Mr. Ralph!" I yelled.

By the time I got to him I was out of breath.

"Are you okay?" He asked.

I nodded my head and put my finger up to let him know that I needed a minute. I was slightly bent over trying to catch my breath.

"Have a seat," he said touching my shoulder.

I jumped aggressively.

"Please don't touch me, I don't like when people touch me!" I shouted.

He threw his hands up and said, "I apologize I didn't mean to offend you. But I'm happy you came back."

"Why is that?"

"I just wanted to thank you. For talking to me and buying me lunch. I can't remember the last time someone held a conversation with me. That meant more to me than the food."

"It doesn't cost anything to be kind," I said.

"No it doesn't, but so many people don't do it. But I can't be upset, because I'm just reaping what I sowed. When I was on top, I didn't ask anyone about their day, because I didn't care."

"Well I'm happy you have learned the error of your ways. But I didn't come to receive any gratification, I came back to give you something."

"I don't need anything else, you've already done more than enough for me."

"Well I'm not the one that gave it to you. I'm just the one giving it to you," I said handing him the care package and the motel room key.

"What is this?" He asked.

"Your opportunity," I said.

"I don't understand."

"The motel up the street has given you a room for 10 days. Tell the desk clerk that the young lady he talked to is your niece. He is the one that blessed you with the room and the care package."

"You told him that I'm your uncle?" Mr. Ralph asked.

"Yes, I apologize for lying. I also told him that tomorrow is your birthday. Aw yeah and he gave me this to," I said as I unzipped my jacket pocket to give him the piece of paper that contained the Outreach Center information.

When I went in my pocket to pull out the paper, I also pulled out seven $5 bills. I was dumbfounded at first because I had no idea where the money came from. Then it dawned on me. Earlier today a man on the train gave me seven $5 bills when he bought $35 worth of snacks from me.

I looked at Mr. Ralph and then looked at the money. Something inside of me was telling me to give it to him. I looked at him once again and then handed it to him with the Outreach information.

"I can't take that Destiny," he said shaking his hands in the air.

"You can and you will. You said you want an opportunity and the desk clerk at the motel gave you one. You said you want someone to gamble on you, well I'm all in. So don't let me down Mr. Ralph. And please don't allow your pride to block your blessings."

I then took his hand and placed the piece of paper and seven $5 bills in his palm, "besides you know what they say about the number seven. It means that positive things are flowing freely toward you at this time."

A tear fell from his eye.

"Sophia used to say that! She used to say, *"positive things are flowing freely, you just have to be open minded to receive it."*

Mr. Ralph could no longer keep it together. He fell to his knees and cried out, "Lord God, You didn't forget about me! Thank You Father, Thank You Jesus, Thank You Lord!!!"

Unfortunately, I couldn't see the beauty in the blessing. All I saw was a grown man crying.

Maybe self-consciously I was irritated because watching him cry and praise God reminded me of that M.A.N. I questioned if Mr. Ralph was mocking God or was he genuinely thankful. I guess it wasn't for me to figure out. That was between him and the God he served.

Mr. Ralph was so busy praising God that he didn't realize that I walked away. But once he noticed I was gone, I was too far for him to reach, so he yelled down the street. "Thank you so much Destiny!"

"You're welcome," I shouted and waved.

Grandma said, "God will put the right people in your life at the right time and for the right reasons."

Once I was sitting comfortably on the train, tears rolled down my face as thoughts flowed through my mind.

I thought about grandma. I missed her so much, I just needed to see her so I could give her a big hug and make sure she was okay. I thought about Mr. Hendrix and how the twenty-seven dollars was the reason I was able to buy and sell snacks. I thought about the manager at Oscar's Dog House and how his rudeness reminded me of the bullies at my school. I thought about Mr. Ralph, and how he genuinely tried to help me when I was out of breath, but I was too damage to accept it. I thought about the manager at the Pizzeria and how he told me I motivated him to be kinder to others. I thought about the desk clerk at the motel and how he was able to bless another homeless man because he knew how it felt to be homeless. I thought about Quinton and how he threw those fries in my face. I thought about Myeisha and how I hadn't talked to her since I accidently injured her. I thought about mom and how she refused to leave her husband. I thought about Ms. Jackson and her unfair punishment. I even thought about Bella and wondered did she miss her father.

In one week I learned so much. I learned that everything happens for a reason. People change so that we can learn to let go, things go wrong so that we can appreciate them when they are right, we believe lies so that we will learn to trust no one but ourselves and God. And sometimes good things fall apart so better things can fall together.

And although I believed that, I was still confused.

And no matter how hard I tried I could not wrap my mind around my situation.

How could I be a blessing to someone else in the midst of their storm, while I was still trying to weather mine? How could I encourage someone else to be strong, when I have lost my own motivation to do so? I'm trying so hard to understand my life so that I could find my peace.

Tears continued to roll down my cheeks. I felt so alone, because not one person noticed my sadness, pain, or silent tears. But I really couldn't be upset, because the truth was…I perfected the skill of masking my pain.

DYING FAITH PROLOGUE

The next morning while I was getting ready for school that M.A.N. approached me. I silently walked around him, but he grabbed my arm.

I snatched away and shouted, "Don't Touch Me!"

"What did you say?" He yelled.

"Chris leave me alone!" I screamed.

"Chris?" He replied shockingly.

"I didn't stutter, utter, or mutter! I will never call you dad again, because Satan doesn't have children!"

"And you don't have a damn daddy. Your father didn't want to be bothered with your ugly ass. That's why he abandoned you. Cause you a dumb bitch."

"Well that makes two dumb bitches. Cause your children don't want to be bothered with your ugly ass either. I don't blame them? Who wants to share DNA with a child molester?" I boldly replied.

My comment upset him.

He grabbed me by my shirt, and bald up his fist.

I dug in my pocket, pulled out my pepper spray, and sprayed him.

He released me and ran in the bathroom to rinse his eyes with cold water.

I quickly grabbed my backpack, ran out the house as fast as I could, and did not stop running until I got to school.

ABOUT THE AUTHOR

Faith Nicole is a mother, an aunt, a teacher, a mentor, an author, and the President of a Nonprofit Organization "Purple Diamonds Inc."

Ms. Faith is no stranger to pain nor struggle. She grew up in Cabrini Green Project Housing and later moved to Chicago's West Side area. After several years she relocated to the South Side of Chicago, to the Englewood neighborhood.

As so many others in the community Faith Nicole witnessed violence first-hand.

However, that was not the only obstacle she was forced to deal with. Due to situations out of her control, she was a victim of an abusive childhood, unfortunately, the abuse continued for years.

Although the abuse came to an end. Ms. Faith's life didn't get any easier. She dealt with other unfortunate situations that made it difficult for her to progress positively. Through her ups, downs, highs, and lows she learned the power of self-love and prayer.

Ms. Faith's belief in God and her will to survive was the reason she was able to conquer each and every trial and tribulation she faced.

Faith Nicole's past did not define her, it pushed her into her, "PURPOSE."

"DYING FAITH"
COMING SOON